Michael Meegan  he received his degree in philosophy from the Milltown Institute of Theology and Philosophy in Dublin. He is a director of the International Community for the Relief of Starvation and Suffering (ICROSS) which has development programmes in South America, India and Africa. He co-ordinates development programmes in East Africa and lives among the Maasai nomads in the Rift Valley. He is currently writing on mystical traditions and the nature of compassion, and trans-lating Maasai for a forthcoming book on Maasai customs and traditions.

All royalties from this book will go towards development programmes among the very poor in East Africa.

MICHAEL MEEGAN

All Shall Be Well

On compassion and love

With a Foreword by
John Powell, S.J.

Collins
FOUNT PAPERBACKS

First published in 1986 by Fount Paperbacks, London

Copyright © Michael Meegan 1986

Made and printed in Great Britain by
William Collins Sons & Co. Ltd,
Glasgow

Bible texts in this volume are
generally the author's own version

Conditions of Sale
This book is sold subject to the condition
that it shall not, by way of trade or otherwise,
be lent, re-sold, hired out or otherwise circulated
without the publisher's prior consent in any form of
binding or cover other than that in which it is
published and without a similar condition
including this condition being imposed
on the subsequent purchaser

This book is humbly dedicated to one of the rarest of men – a simple and hidden man who radiates love and compassion wherever he goes. He is one of those rare priests of heaven who plays in his father's garden, as a child.

To Father Paul Cunningham
With love

Contents

Foreword	9
Acknowledgements	13
Introduction	15
One A World Unloved	17
Two We Stand Alone	33
Three Our Deepest Hope	46
Four In Search of the Sacred	65
Five Christ, the Gentle Lover	84
Six The Sacred Within	105
Seven The Dynamic Response	128
Eight All Shall Be Well	145
Reflections and Prayers	149
Bibliography	158

Foreword

I have always wanted to be heroic. I have always wanted to do something significant with the life and gifts God has given me. I have wanted to leave this world better than I found it. There is a restless part of me that seeks the wholeness and holiness of the saints. Unfortunately, the older I get the more I come into contact with my fragility. I must face the fact that I am a fraction. My goodness is mixed with weakness. My weakness is somehow mixed with goodness.

I think that I have projected my interior desire for a personal heroism into looking for heroes. Someone has rightly said that what we are speaks so loudly that others can't hear what we say. I keep looking for those people who live the Christian vision I have been preaching, teaching and writing about. I think of them as my role models.

Several years ago I started corresponding with the author of this book, Michael Meegan. He is a member of ICROSS, the "International Community for the Relief of Starvation and Suffering". He is currently working with the starving sick and suffering in East Africa.

From the beginning, Michael's words stirred the embers of my desire to look for and find the living witnesses of the Christian legacy. My own coldness has always sought the warmth of people who really care, who take seriously the words of Jesus: "I was hungry and you gave me to eat. I was thirsty and you gave me to drink. I was sick and you cared for me."

Michael's letters usually came wrapped around several

Foreword

photographs. It is true, I think, that very often a picture is worth a thousand words. There – in several of those pictures – was my friend Michael, with a dead child in his arms. The sadness and compassion in his face, and the tenderness with which he held this little victim of starvation, moved me very deeply. I would often sit staring at these pictures and thinking deeply about the words that Michael had written. I would silently think to myself: "You are my hero, Michael."

I must be honest with you and admit that I do not think I would be capable of what this young man is doing. The sadness of sickness and starvation, and, I would think, the "endlessness of it all", would consume me, burn me out. I think I can only admire the Michael Meegans of this world from a safe distance. My fragile fraction would not sustain the enormous burdens of human suffering that Michael deals with daily.

Strangely enough, the letters of Michael reflected optimism and hope, rather than futility and burnout. He often wrote of the quiet, inner dignity of the African people with whom he was working. Their values seemed to be more in place than the values of the affluent. Their grinding poverty had deprived them of everything except an inner peace that comes from knowing what is important and what is unimportant.

There was another feature of Michael's letters that always astonished me: his own quiet optmism that, in the title of his book, "All Shall Be Well". He seemed somehow to live with a deep sense of compassion, and to integrate it with a peaceful sense that God would some day write straight with our crooked lines. Michael is confident that in the end love will triumph over greed, compassion over cruelty. His book will certainly be a great contribution to that end.

My own sense of responsibility for this world is a painful challenge at times. There are so many unheard cries of

Foreword

pain, so many bleeding wounds in need of bandaging. Sometimes I feel that I am a pain-filled personification of that saying: "Lord, the sea is so wide and my boat is so small."

At such times of personal ego desperation, I think of people like Michael Meegan and the members of ICROSS. Suddenly, the world feels much warmer and the sky looks much brighter. I see those gentle hands and that compassionate face. I see the members of ICROSS holding tiny human beings gently in the hands of love. Every experience becomes a memory to be carried through life, and I am aware that every such act of human compassion and love will never die as long as there is a human memory to cherish it.

Finally, I am convinced that a loving God has sent each one of us into this world with a special message to deliver, a special song to sing, and a special act of love to bestow. Whether that message, song and act of love will reach only a few or many depends on the will of God. Michael Meegan's message, song and act of love have moved and continue to move me profoundly. So I have asked him to share it with others in writing. The result has been this book which you are now holding in your hands. I hope that it will affect you as deeply as it has influenced me. I hope he will come across as effectively in these pages as he has come over land and sea in his letters to me.

Lastly, there are strong refrains of human exhortation in these pages. If you are like me, you do not want to be exhorted by someone who knows only the word-level of compassion and love. Such appeals suggest manipulation rather than a true appeal. I know that I am successfully challenged by those who have risen to the challenge themselves. And that is one reason why Michael Meegan's words are more than words to me. His love and compassion are like perpetual flames that burn in the distant night. And by the light of those flames the world I live in

Foreword

seems much brighter. By the warmth of those flames my world feels much warmer.

Once upon a time a small boy offered Jesus five loaves of bread and two fish to feed a hungry multitude that must have numbered fifteen thousand people. (Five thousand people, but that was not counting women and children.) The gift was so small compared to the number of empty stomachs and reaching hands. Yet in the hands of the Lord, the small gift multiplied. And all were filled.

Somehow I am sure that Michael Meegan and those who labour with him to alleviate the sickness and suffering of God's less fortunate are like that little boy. What they hold out will be multiplied in the loving hands of God which reach out to accept the gift gratefully. Their lives will draw down upon this world a shower of God's grace: a shower that will wash down this hot, sick and tired world. And this shower will result in a new fertility of our human soil, a new springtime for our human hearts.

Thank you, Michael: for your great heart and your beautiful book.

Loyola University of Chicago John Powell, S.J
February, 1986

Acknowledgements

My thanks to Father Albert, Cistercian, for his friendship and kindness, and to Father Corbett Walsh, S.J. for his many insights into the gentleness of Christ.

I am indebted to Father Brendan O'Brien's encyclopedic knowledge of Scripture. Father Paul Lennon O'Carn has over the years provided much support and scholarly advice.

Thanks also go to my colleagues, especially Dr Joe Barnes, Vincent Kenny and Dr Tom O'Riordan, and our many friends, without whom our work in Africa would be impossible. A special word of thanks to Des Rughe for his vision and vitality and to my parents, without whom I wouldn't be here.

Much is owed to Sarah Baird-Smith, who has guided me throughout the writing of this book, and to the many who live and work with me – may our gentle Lord bless you.

Introduction

A dear friend of mine and a source of constant support, John Powell, S.J., encouraged me to try to write. A few months later the subject of the book was defined when Toby Eady wrote: "I have one word to say to you. Write a book about love, otherwise the rest of life is pointless."

What can I tell you about love other than what you already know? Perhaps our shared failures and doubts, hopes and visions, might encourage and enrich each other. The book is born of my own experience of prayer and silence. It comes from me, it comes from Africa.

As I write, there is a little boy sitting by the typewriter on the desk. He needs clothes, he needs shelter, he needs food. What ultimately matters is how we live, and how much we really care. Theory must be lived out, the books must eventually be put down and we must got out to our brothers and sisters, and touch them, be with them and love each other . . .

This is the only thing that matters, the very reason we live.

I think they will remember this as the age of lamentations,
The age of broken minds and broken souls,
The age of hurt creatures sobbing out their sorrow to the
    rhythm of the blues –
The music of lost Africa's desolation become the music of
    the town.

The age of failure of splendid things,
The age of the deformity of splendid things,
The age of old young men and bitter children,
The age of treachery and of a great new faith.
The age of madness and machines,
Of broken bodies and fear–twisted hearts,

The age of frenzied fumbling and possessive lusts –
And yet, deep down, an age unsatisfied by dirt and guns,
An age which though choked by the selfishness of the few
    who owned their bodies and their souls,
Still struggled blindly to the end,
And in their time reached out magnificently
Even for the very stars themselves.

H. D. CARBERRY

CHAPTER ONE

A World Unloved

In the beginning, all creation was loved into being. He made rare and hidden things full of light and beauty. He smiled through the mystery, and even the darkness was filled with his sweetness.

Then, with great joy, his love conceived its most beautiful miracle of all, his most treasured creation, and so from the dawn of time he carried you in his heart until now. Nothing in creation is more beautiful or more loved than you – nothing could ever take your place in his heart.

Within you lies the purest power of all, the seed of tenderness and love. If for a single moment we saw how intimately we are cherished and held in his arms, fear would be banished for ever and our faces would reflect his warmth and his joy always.

This book is about the celebration of life, the miracle of the dance and the victory of light. It is about gentleness in a world that is in pain, it is about real people living in a real world.

There is a war being fought – a war between good and evil, between healing and hurting. The battles are on every level, cosmic, global, social. There is conflict in our media, our jobs and our homes, but more urgently the conflict is within ourselves.

The ultimate issues of good and evil, love and hate, embrace us all. Humanity is such that we sometimes fight on both sides of the war. It often seems that evil is winning, there is so much corruption and greed in the world. These days we have a lot of bad news and rarely do we hear how vibrant and active love really is.

All Shall Be Well

We are afraid, we hide the most precious things within us most of the time for fear they will be hurt. We share our friendship and trust with but a few and rarely do we enfold each other in the wings of love and the intimacy of ourselves.

Our home and breath is love itself and the image in which we were made to rejoice and cherish all things. Love's hands brought the world together but the tragedy was that mankind's fears tore it apart.

If we believe in the dawn of a happier day and that we are the co-authors of a better world, then we must descend to the bowels of the earth as well as soar to the heights of God. If we are to strive for a gentler world, we must as well see the shame and sorrow of a torn and anxious world, the world of today.

Our earth is stained in blood, divided by hatred and blinded by greed; it is a world worried about tomorrow, uncertain of today, and guilty of yesterday. It is an earth unsatisfied and frightened of itself.

No mysticism or thrust towards the sacred can be made without the blood of the innocent, the tears of broken mothers, the violence of humanity. We cannot walk into the darkness towards the answer without our hearts and souls being aware of the shame and futility of a world gone hopelessly wrong. We've never been more aware of the problems that face us, nor of the sadism, cruelty and needless suffering in the world.

I do not believe we will ever get used to famine or torture or violence, because any form of cruelty and injustice is wrong no matter what label is put upon it and no matter for what cause it is done. Looking at suffering tends to frighten us; the sight of pain or hunger of dying people tends to conjure up all sorts of fears, preconceptions. How much more disturbing would it be were we to look upon a whole world which is crippled, which is in pain.

A World Unloved

There is a story that tells of a little island in the midst of a great ocean. On the island there lived two families. They had everything they could ever possibly need, so much so that they sent food to other parts of the world from their great ports. But after many years there came a famine on one half of the island and it became dry and wasted; over the mountain on the other side, food grew and they prospered. Those who had much sat together to see how they might be able to help the other half on the other side of the hill. They talked, and one of them said: "If we feed our children on the other side of the hill they will become lazy, they will beg from us and will not want to work." Another said: "They are the same blood as us and we are of the same land. We are one family and there is no difference between us. We must share what we have." And so the elders spoke for many days, each one in his turn.

At length they decided to go to the coffers of the town, and with great pomp and ceremony they took the silver coin from one of the golden caskets. After the elders went to their families and explained the importance of helping their relatives on the other side of the hill, a delegation was sent to present the silver coin to the other family. But most of the people didn't really understand because they had never been to the other side of the hill. When the elders climbed at last to the top they glanced at each other in amazement, for there before them lay the other half of the island, empty and deserted. They stood on the hilltop for a long time until the light faded and darkness came. They turned homeward with tears in their eyes.

On our little island there are over 500 million of our children slowly starving to death while we on our half of the island ponder what to do about them. We prosper. We have far more than we need, so much that there are great mountains of spare food.

There is no violence worse than poverty. Since the

All Shall Be Well

magnitude of poverty is beyond our imagination, let us turn away from the statistics for a moment.

A boy I once knew, Camillo, was about fifteen years old and he had lost his father. So he helped his mother to look after the other children. They were able to grow just enough food to feed themselves; they had known what it meant to sleep without eating. But when the rains failed again their crops died and they had nothing to eat. The family joined hundreds of friends and relations to look for help, and as they walked through the barren desert the hundreds grew into thousands, and the thousands grew into hundreds of thousands. Despite those who were old and weak and crippled who died on the way, the hundreds of thousands slowly grew into millions.

Many were settled in camps; most of the young children became very sick with stomach trouble. Finally Camillo and his family came upon some water which was stale and stagnant. It was a choice of letting the children become even more dehydrated or quenching their thirst with filthy water. So Camillo and his mother let the children drink. A few weeks later, in a refugee camp, the three youngest children died of chronic diarrhoea and dehydration.

Camillo himself was eventually turned out of the camp as he did not qualify for famine relief. His mother remained with the other two children, with one sheet between them to cover them at night. The boy went begging from village to village. He sold his two sheets for food. His sandals had been stolen in the camp, and over the coming weeks he was to waste away and to become only sixty pounds in weight. His hair slowly fell out and his physique changed from that of a handsome athlete to a pathetic skeleton, from an intelligent and attractive young man with a future to a pitiful statistic barely able to talk.

Hunger is the most dreadful way to die. It is slow and gradual, and it is the result of many things. But whatever way the experts care to put it, the result is the same –

A World Unloved

degrading and humiliating. And when you see them taking a photograph of you, then you see you are too far gone to be helped.

Before Camillo came to us he had walked over two hundred miles and found a small boy whom he brought with him. He had to keep spitting into the boy's mouth to keep it from becoming dry and swollen. Camillo's face had withered into that of an old man. He died simply from exhaustion and lack of food. He never knew what it was to go to school, to have nice clothes, to have a girlfriend or to watch television. He never had his own things. He knew what it was like to have nowhere to go, to have no water to give his little brothers and sisters. He knew the meaning of hunger. The picture of Camillo still haunts me. One could write a book on him alone, on his gratitude, his haunting eyes, and, despite all the misery and tragedy that came his way, despite everything, his wonderful smile.

On the projections of the statistics about the agonies of so many people like Camillo and his mother, the present famine in Africa will kill some ten million people, but it is only a prelude to an inevitable further famine, a worse crisis. "More people may die in Africa as a result of this present famine, than died in the First World War," said F. Bradford Moose of the United Nations. And throughout the world more and more children still go hungry.

We are often disillusioned and frustrated when we hear that so much aid and effort is being wasted and misused by corrupt authorities and is falling into the wrong hands. But when a child is starving does one withhold food to punish a corrupt government? Does one give up simply because of the odds? A two-month-old baby abandoned in a cardboard box isn't interested in religion, politics or strategy. She only wants to be fed, to be warm and to be loved.

There can be no fear worse than being abandoned and outcast, totally unwanted, with nowhere to go, stateless, trapped in a corridor that inevitably leads to a degrading and humiliating death, dumped upon a human rubbish heap. The alternatives are pitifully limited. Either the poor shall come to their end somewhere along the road, under a tree, under a cardboard box, or huddled under a blanket, or they shall perhaps be rescued for a time by charity.

Of the six million refugees in Africa today, more than half are children, and despite the countless reports, studies and efforts from the Western world, we simply cannot feed the majority of the world's population from the crumbs off our table. Feeding some of the children is not enough. We must ask why they continue to be hungry and in greater numbers each year. Archbishop Helder Camara said: "When I give food to the starving, they call me a saint. But when I ask why they have no food, they call me a Communist."

Many of those who survive the ravages and cruelties of famine and drought, and the countless infectious diseases, are permanently scarred. The damage done to today's little children will cripple tomorrow. Most effects of malnutrition are imperceptible. They aren't just in the wasted limbs and the deformed heads and the dehydrated skin.

One of the boys who lives with us now was seriously malnourished as an infant. There was not enough food to feed all the children, so some were more neglected than others. The weakest were usually left out. When this boy did get some food, he would sit alone in a corner. Now, some years later, he rarely speaks and sometimes wakes up at night crying, apparently for no reason. He is shy, nervous, uneasy; there are periods when he is so fearful he can neither eat nor talk for days, sometimes a week, and he spends hours staring into space, sleeping with both arms defensively about his head. At times his memories of hunger and sickness overflow into hysteria. He will always be afraid, always be marked. With a great deal of time and patience we may be able to heal some of his wounds, but a great deal of damage has been done. A few months ago his youngest brother died from malnutrition and from diarrhoea.

The extremities of life that beset most of mankind are beyond our conception and so are unreal for us. Words like "Famine" and "starvation" are simply empty words. The rock singer, Bob Geldof, recently addressed some international stars and beautifully illustrated the point. "I don't know if we can conceive of nothing, but nothing is not having a cardboard box to sleep under in minus ten degrees. Nothing is not just having no drink to get drunk on, but not having any water. Nothing is a child squatting in its own diarrhoea."

One of the great fears is that the West is slowly becoming immune to the intensive famine coverage. If we continue to treat famine as a dramatic news item, we shall never face or deal with the real problems. Unless our vision goes further than disaster relief and Band-Aid, we shall always permit a state of prefamine suffering for the billions of people who live in the Third and Fourth Worlds, and we will always accept a social system of haves and have-nots, a system essentially unjust.

Unless we ourselves adopt a new set of priorities, the future of Africa, India and South America is an inevitable and terrifying one of incalculable consequences. Theories and strategies can go so far, powerful media photography can touch us just so much, but change doesn't come from outside. It comes from the recognition of some common reservoir of life and compassion that we all possess, a presence within us all that lies trembling somewhere in our hearts, that needs awakening.

When the philosopher and anthropologist, Bronowski, was asked what he thought was the greatest danger facing mankind, he fell silent for a long time. His answer was not nuclear holocaust, neither was it capitalism or Communism, or world food shortages, or over-population.

All Shall Be Well

Yet the depth and simplicity of his response embraced the sum total of human folly. He said that the greatest threat facing mankind today was that "man stands in imminent danger of losing his own spirituality and, in doing so, losing his identity". It is like the rich man who spoke to Jesus and wanted to know what he could do to become a better person – in the end he couldn't really pay the price of what Jesus was asking, and he went away sad. Yet the most important part of that story is that he went away and Jesus still loved him.

We like what we own and we'd like to have more, but somewhere within the web of modern life our children are being brought up to believe in material gain, in a philosophy of possessive values, where this is mine and that is yours and I will do what I want with mine. Such an ideology always makes the poor poorer and the rich richer and everybody dissatisfied. But there is a poverty in materialism too, no matter how much one owns, because no matter what one has one will never be fully satisfied.

Such a value system is based on getting more and better, on advancing, and such an upward mobility inevitably reaches stalemate. But not everyone is possessive and those who give to the poor are usually poor themselves – like the story of the rich Pharisee in the temple who made a great show of giving many gold coins, when in the shadows the humble widow slipped in her few pennies, giving all that she had.

A story was told by one of our doctors who spent most of his life among the very poor. One night he got a note from two sisters who lived in the inner city, asking him to visit them because they wanted so much to see him and help him with his work. He finally got round to visiting, late one evening, and he found a tiny little back room in a tenement building. The windows were broken, there was no electricty, and the slum was almost deserted and ridden with rats.

A World Unloved

One of the old women was bed-ridden and the other had no teeth, was half bald and almost blind. They had a small radio held together with Sellotape, a broken mug on the table, and lots of cats which gave the room its distinctive smell. The plaster was falling off the ceiling. With great glee and delight the two old sisters handed him a little bundle wrapped carefully in a small envelope. They had read an article in one of the newspapers and had saved some of their pension, their coins and notes, and wanted, as they put it, "to help the poor". Such stories tend to rekindle one's faith in human nature.

Sadly, however, materialism and commercialism seem to outweigh the little deeds by little people. In such a busy world we don't have much time or patience. We put our old people into homes and the mentally handicapped into institutions. Things tend to become black and white for us and we have no time to look too deeply. We unwittingly do something that Christ never did – we start to judge each other and to look at *what* people are, not who they are. We see a black man or a Hispanic, a prostitute or a homosexual. We don't see the person, neither do we give them much time.

We are even conditioned to judge ourselves, our appearances and our level of success by a television value system that persuades its viewers that they need the lastest fashions. Advertising so deeply controls its audience that they believe themselves poor and deprived if their wants are not fulfilled and their imaginary needs not satisfied. We live in an age that has thus become frightened of itself.

We have grown essentially afraid – afraid of the problems and violence that surround us, of the pressures and demands laid upon us by the city life. We are afraid of being hurt and rejected, of being unwanted and unloved. We have grown afraid of what we have become, afraid even to love; and worst of all, we are afraid of ourselves.

We hear every day of hate and intolerance, of bomb

blasts and hijacking, of murders and suicides. We have never been so in touch with the pulse of human misery as now. In such a world it is easy to close one's eyes and ignore it all; it is easy to reject a God who allows young men to be tortured and sodomized in prison, a world that has now devised its own destruction of itself, by itself.

In El Salvador a young woman and child were bayoneted. In India they played football with babies who were thrown to the ground and kicked to death. In London a gang murdered an old couple after torturing them. In New York a fifteen year old girl was raped and cut open by a group of boys. She died in hospital a few days later, terrified. According to Amnesty International, torture is used in many countries worldwide by men who humiliate and seek to degrade other men.

In almost every city, in every corner of the world, there are unwanted and neglected people who live from rubbish bins, from our waste scraps; they sleep in doorways and beg for pennies because we have no room for them in our society.

To see us as we really are, hurts; the poverty and injustice hurt. Where do we stand in such a confused and unequal world? Insecure and questioning? Where do we begin our search? Where is God? Between two golden candlesticks upon the cathedral's high altar? Or has he fled and left us to ourselves? We are crying out and searching for a way – a reason. We stand on the brink of a precipice in the midst of a hurting family. In the silence of our hearts we hear the cries of the hungry.

There is a story that tells of a mystic and a boy. For hours they stood upon the rooftop staring at the great city below. The old man rested like some ancient statue, and the boy's dark eyes shone in the night. Their words were few and as darkness fell the boy looked upon the figure in the shadows, hooded by the veil of night.

A World Unloved

The boy, like all boys, had a thousand questions in his heart, but the old man bade him wait for a while. From the shadows the bowed figure moved into the light and the boy saw that the old man's eyes were full of tears. He looked upon the boy so full of wonder, touched his hand and bade him close his eyes so as to see into the night.

The old man showed the boy the life within the city below.

They saw a man, who was very drunk and was arguing with his wife. He pulled her from the bed and dragged her to the kitchen so that she could make some food for him. She was crying for him to stop. Then two children came downstairs to see what was going on. There was a girl about ten years old and a boy about eight. The man began shouting at them. The little boy told him to leave his mother alone. The man was furious and, knocking the girl aside, he grabbed the boy and dragged him upstairs. He stripped him and beat him all around the room. The mother and the young girl sat in the corner of the kitchen crying.

The boy on the rooftop clenched his fist in anger and opened his eyes breaking the silence. "For God's sake stop!" he cried, but he was far away on the other side of the city. He turned to the old man, his face anxious and searching, but the mystic remained silent. He merely wiped the beads of sweat upon the boy's brown forehead and closed the great dark oceans that were his eyes.

After some time the boy began to see the slums and the nightlife, the nightclubs and the highrise flats. The heart of the old man found a grey tenement. In the basement a kid stuck a syringe into his forearm and slowly filled himself with dope. There was a girl in a doorway; she was young, she had no job during the day so she worked at night selling herself for twenty dollars. They saw her eyes close as a stranger mauled her body and opened her clothes, and as he touched her she whispered in her shame.

All Shall Be Well

Far away the mystic felt the loneliness of an old woman as she sat alone in her little room – her friends had all gone, she was scared to go out. It was nighttime and despite the neon lights she was afraid and it was very dark . . .

"Do you want to see more?" asked the old man, his eyes still closed. "No, I don't want to see all this stuff", replied the boy. But after some time he opened his great dark eyes to look at the old man, whose closed eyes still hid the tears within. The boy rested against the air conditioning vent, one leg against the wall, still hand in hand with the bowed figure. Without a word they walked once again through the streets below as the old man's heart searched and looked for humanity.

A black boy had just walked his girlfriend home – she lived in a white neighbourhood. On the way back he was picked up by the police who accused him of trying to steal from a shop about an hour or so before. Very frightened, he stood up against the wall in the police station and a small, angry looking man started to strike the boy's face with the back of his hand. The boy was handcuffed from behind. They told him to sign a statement. He politely refused. He was slapped again and he began to taste blood in his mouth. He was terrified of the three policemen who stood around him. He felt a blow to his stomach and doubled up. He was made to stand, legs apart, and the statement was signed after the small man lifted his knee between the boy's legs once then twice. He squatted that night in a corner of the cell, his jeans stained with blood, and weeping with no one to hear him.

It was almost morning and brightness touched a corner of the night. The old man was mantled in the mists of dawn, his white hair entwined with the sun. In wonder the boy looked over the city – he was filled with sorrow and anger, helplessness and pain, and from his wounds tears fell on soft brown cheeks.

It was now a new morning. Below the horns and sirens,

A World Unloved

the hum of traffic hustled blindly into the day. No one looked up and saw the moon and her train of stars; no one gazed at the red orb of the sun as he climbed high to cast his warmth upon the earth; and still no one saw the young boy upon the high roof, or, at his side, the old man.

If we look with our hearts and feel with our souls something begins to change inside us. Our insight into humanity becomes unity and feeling and emotion, and when we see the pain and suffering of another we begin to feel as one of them. All of us, like the young boy, feel the frustration and helplessness in a world so big and at times so unwelcoming. It is understandable in such a world that so many have rejected a God, institutional religions and formal prayer, and that somehow they have lost hope in the future, are full of doubt and confusion.

The tragedy of such a world is that we begin merely to survive and exist, not live and rejoice. We function, do our work well, but the world begins to revolve around ourselves and the limits of our own immediate activities – vision and wonder starve within us and happiness becomes lost.

Happiness is one of those strange inner gifts; it is not bought or learnt, it simply seems to be there. One night I was trying to think of an example to illustrate the point. There was a knock on the door. It was very cold and very late, and we wondered who it was. Then in trailed a rather bedraggled, anxious young woman with a baby at her breast, and a small girl who couldn't have been more than four years old whose name was Ndito. The young mother sat on my bed, the little girl squatting on the floor smiling at me. They were all covered in dust and filth. The mother wore a dirty torn sheet, the little girl wore nothing.

The story unravelled – the history of the woman's life. If the mother had been born in America, she would undoubtedly have been in high school by now, thinking of

All Shall Be Well

where to go in her summer holidays and what to add to her record collection; the little girl might be in nursery, toddling home to watch television, carrying her teddy bear with her. Instead, here they were, cold and pathetic, in a small wooden clinic out in the middle of the desert. I felt helpless and miserable. They were thin and ill, with no clothes, no money, no home, no food, not even a blanket, on top of which the drought and famine didn't help. Ndito had lost interest in the conversation. She had joined the boys in the corner of the room.

By the time I had listened to the whole story and checked all we had in the stores, the baby had relieved himself all over the bed. The mother was almost in tears. One of the boys had wrapped Ndito up in our one and only tablecloth, much to her delight.

I looked over at the little girl – she had nothing on earth, not even a place to lay her head for the night, and yet she was beaming with delight, her eyes full of joy. Then it dawned on me that she had that gift of happiness inside – it was just there.

Some parts of me felt warmed by her, another part wanted to pick her up and keep her. As they began the journey next morning Ndito carried a little toy doll that one of the boys had given her and a bundle of food. At least they had drunk from our little stream on their journey.

We live at a time when mankind is discovering more wonderful things than ever, yet it is also the time of sorrow. As we have mentioned, the world has never had so many homeless, hungry children. Yet while two-thirds of humanity live in tremendous poverty, many of us have more wealth than we know what to do with. We have invested enormous amounts of world resources in devising new, improved ways of mass destruction and in creating bombs that will wiped out human beings without destroying the environment.

A World Unloved

In a world so divorced from itself it is not surprising that human society has become unhealthy and has developed symptoms reflecting its profound distress. For example, according to the United States Institute of Mental Health, 10 million Americans are classified as mentally ill. A conservative estimate is that some 35,000 successful suicides occur each year, with approximately 450,000 attempted suicides. The second highest cause of infant deaths in the United States is child abuse; over 5 per cent of the adult population in America is alcoholic. According to the World Health Organization, the world's greatest health problem is depression and stress.

When all we hear about is violence, wars, corruption, it is not surprising that alcoholism, violence and personal mental illness occur. In an age so divided and overwhelmed it is no wonder that so many people prefer to retreat into self-security rather than risk facing challenges and discoveries.

In such a torn environment we close our doors at night, and yet the world follows us into our living rooms. No matter how indifferent we try to be, we are moved by human pain. We will always be hurt by suffering; something in us is touched by all the hunger and all the misery, and we do not know where to turn. The essential tragedy is that in our own attempt to survive we bury so much of the beauty that is within us, trying to protect and hide our fragile selves so that we irreparably cripple the potential and the energy and the love that lie within us waiting to be shared.

We do not know where to go or where to turn. We have become cautious and sceptical, not only of those around us but of every facet of our lives. We have become cynical of the gods proposed by institutional religions. We do not need a judgemental Lord to punish us, a God who remembers our sins and who gets offended at the least weakness. We do not need a solemn mystery owned and taught by theologians, neither do we need to be preached at by those who are holier than us who have monopolized God. We have rejected such human concepts of God so that all too often we fill the gap with an equally confusing and dead substitute.

Many people feel abandoned and deserted. Where is God for a young beggar picking up grains of rice from the dirt? Where is the quality and dignity of life for a baby born into squalor and disease, who dies a month later never having known a full stomach? Where was hope for the terrified young woman in a gas chamber? What is at the end of the lonely despair of a deserted old woman living in a tiny room awaiting a better world? We are in need of emotional and social healing, spiritual revolution, and discovery of the reasons for life. We need a noticeable shift in values and priorities to allow us to be more alive.

We need to be liberated from the pain of the world – a liberation not of ideas, but of deeds, not of policies but of love.

CHAPTER TWO

We Stand Alone

The feeling of helplessness and frustration in the face of staggering odds is a common enough reaction to today's problems. We sometimes live "our daily lives perilously close to the brink of absurdity and despair" (Andrew Greeely, *The Great Mysteries*).

We stand wide-eyed, wondering, wondering what it's all about. Each of us has known those moments of confusion and apprehension. Just as we have all felt times of great delight, we have stood offended and uncertain at the wrong and evil that live in the world. The raw human pain shudders around us in a trembling hand, an angry voice, a rebuff, an unwanted child. Where do we stand in such a world amid such turbulence and division?

How we respond to the world raging all about us largely depends upon two factors and their integration into our lives.

The first factor is the way in which we see reality around us. This is influenced by the society that we live in, by its moral codes, by family and friends, by media and religion.

The most important factor, which affects everything we do and say, is how we see ourselves. The harmony that is in each person comes both from the set of values by which he measures humanity and himself and also an interior life – one's own personal spirituality.

Essentially there are two ways in which we evaluate what is around us. Firstly we see, the world and everything in it; and here we can react with a degree of

All Shall Be Well

objectivity. Secondly we react in the context of the world's immediacy upon our lives; this is subjective response.

In order to examine the complexity of our lives, it is important that we look briefly at the human crisis today. Honest selfgrowth only occurs after we begin to understand more about our own feelings and emotions, through awareness of our selfvision and our hopes. The beginning of understanding comes when, freeing ourselves from fear and self-doubt, we begin to learn to love ourselves.

It is important that we see a valid reason and purpose to what at times seems the dull, meaningless monotony of life. Crucial to our growth is a healthy perception of life so that it makes some sort of sense. In our ignorance we sometimes get diverted and end up in addictions, obsessions or other cul-de-sacs which started out as possible shortcuts to a happy life.

If I am to think and grow with maturity, much depends upon a balance that must be attained between myself and others. The internal balance required for human understanding is not so much intellectual as intuitive. It is a blending of common sense with gut instinct. Though it sometimes might help, a psychology degree does not teach me the art of understanding; understanding comes from interacting with each other, enjoying each other, and listening, feeling, sensing; it comes straight from the heart.

We all need to be understood, and it hurts like hell if someone does not understand us. So, a bit like tortoises, we grow a shell in which we can hide in moments of pain and vulnerability. We hide from those who bully and intimidate us, those we hate and those we love. We hide in our lives from the senseless events and mindless tragedies that fill the world. Worst of all, we hide from ourselves.

We try to understand in many ways; we read books, but they don't quite seem to give answers. We don't find the consolation we are looking for because often our channels

We Stand Alone

of communication and reception are either closed or clogged up. Not only does this cause much of our frustration, but this sort of communication difficulty can also mean the crippling and destruction of friendships and close relationships.

Among those thinkers who have made tremendous contributions are Reuel Howe, Victor Frankyl, Erich Fromm and John Powell, all of whom centre their theses upon two simple insights: that we are essentially good and that we are made to love.

Life begins with the immediacy of me, myself, my feelings and pains. It is anchored to my daily experiences and related to those around me. But John Powell's book, *Why Am I Afraid to Love?* says that though life starts with the recognition of my own life and experience, the fullness of my life lies in the hope that it does not end in me. If we do not grow outwards and upwards we remain stunted like a dwarfed tree that has never seen the sunlight.

If we end the discovery of life, we are in a sense already dead; we have adopted a life principle of self-centredness. The meaning of humanity, the meaning and richness of me, is that I can grow into an outgoing, caring person. We are wonderful, free solitudes, who can touch and celebrate and fill each other.

Real discovery begins with the belief that I could be a better person, that there is room for more love, more forgiveness in my life. True human growth begins by the desire to be better than we are and kinder than we have been. It starts when we begin to appreciate ourselves and to educate ourselves into a deeper awareness. Inevitably questions arise from our deepening. As we get older, we become more concious of time and age, of life direction, meaning and value. We face suffering and death, all too often we have no one to help us prise out our very personal thoughts. It is important to be wide awake if we are going

All Shall Be Well

to live our dreams into reality. Fortunately there are downtoearth thinkers who have cast much light on the personal search as we strive to be human, who encourage us to love and search.

A lot of life is very contradictory for us. It is hard to forgive God for giving us a handicapped child or for letting someone we love die and leaving us desolate. All the little misunderstandings and silences, rows and hurts of family life can be very damaging. "The treason of friends, the envy of neighbours – such tragedies, some large, some very small, seem to be without pattern or intent," says Andrew Greeley.

The question of life is so large, so overwhelming, that most of us content ourselves with the little pleasures of living, a quiet drink with friends, a pleasant meal, a stroll down Main Street. It is easier and much less painful not to look too far beyond the horizons of our situation. We try not to ask too many questions in case we might stumble accidentally upon the answer. But there is too much goodness in us not to be moved at all the need around us, and inevitably we question ourselves "Why didn't we help, why didn't we try, why . . . ?"

From time to time our search for meaning becomes a thirst for immediate understanding. When one's mother or father is dying, or when one is close to death, a million thoughts and longings explode into one's mind. We need to talk, but so often there is no one there whom we can talk with, no one who speaks the same language. We grasp into the darkness and wonder – are we alone?

The journey towards a celebration of other people and the attitude of tenderness and caring, is a painful and demanding pilgrimage that involves a humility and tenacity. There is a phrase in the Scriptures referring to the service of God: "Put your hand to the plough and don't turn back." A friend of mine, who spent his life

We Stand Alone

among the slums of Third World cities, told me that sometimes he was hanging on to the plough with both hands, at other times pulling it himself, while at other times he just left it for a while. The plough is really our journey through life, it is the sowing of the seeds of hope. One of the frustrations when sowing such seeds is that we sometimes don't see the beautiful flowers that grow, we only see the hard, lonely, messy work of laying the seed. Our efforts appear just like a big pile of mud, yet in time from nothing grows the most beautiful and perfect of flowers.

We need to give of ourselves if we are to become the full potential that God in his extraordinary and irrational generosity wanted us to be. Inside us there is a miracle. If you have ever seen the ocean and how vast it is, or the desert and how endless it is, or looked up and seen the galaxy, which to our minds is almost infinite, close your eyes and remember that the power of love that exists inside you is even greater than all of the universe. It is deeper and wider than the created world and expands into eternity just as you will expand into eternity in the life that you have been promised with God. The essential sadness of humanity is that many of us live without realizing the promise and gift of God, that as his children we will inherit the deepest and fullest joy of all, which is to love each other and the source of love for ever.

If we do not see inside ourselves the gift of life and the promise of being loved always, life turns into a rather urbane existence full of trivia and pettiness; it remains unsanctified by the fullness of God, for we see but we cannot feel what we see. We become selfish, or rather we cease to become ourselves when we allow defences and fears to block our journey.

Sometimes we feel hurt by others, they reject what they see. It's much better for them to reject the façade we build than the real us; it is better for them to see the cold walls of

All Shall Be Well

our exterior than the little us that dwells within. After all, in our heart of hearts we're all we've got.

If I see no goodness in myself I won't like being myself, and my wounds will fester and deepen inside until they overflow into my life, or I will live in a world of self-deception and pretension. Most of us to a greater or lesser extent are coloured by the opinions of others. Sometimes we go to extreme lengths to satisfy the judgements and views of those around us; we conform, compromise, and play the game. But if the game is just to gain acceptance, it becomes a burden and a role-play, not the life that we were promised, not the vision to be ascended to.

Like fish, we find it easier to swim together. If we stop to reflect long enough, we realize that very little of our own lives is actually a projection of our real selves, but more the mirror of what others would like us to be or expect us to be. When a child is born among the Maasai, among the blessings and prayers bestowed upon the tiny infant is *"Taa A'ke iye"* (Be your full self). This we can only be if we are given and cultivate a rich and whole image of ourselves, and if we see all the wonder and beauty that we are.

Self-image is basically who we perceive ourselves to be, how we see ourselves, our personal worth, the confidence we place in our own integrity and being. It is the sum total of our "us" to ourselves. Though it is sometimes influenced by how we perform, how well we do things, it is built on foundations that were laid from our earliest years. If our self-image is at the mercy of the fluctuating opinions of others, we shall always be capricious and trying to please their varying and exacting demands.

All too often, we try to buy into friendships and confidences. If we have been conditioned by society to believe that we have no value or worth in ourselves, we will extend that depreciation to everything else about us. We will become cynical and sarcastic, masks that transparently cover a discontented self. Most psychiatrists agree, the affection and love given in early childhood shapes the course of future feelings and relationships. All of us see the results of parental love in the first few years of life of those around us.

In the extreme temperatures of sub-Saharan Africa there live countless thousands of poor pastoral nomads scattered over the great rift valley and the plains beyond. One such family lives in a tiny hut made from cardboard boxes and packing cases. This is the home for nine children and their mother, an old woman. The mother spends most of her day finding firewood and carrying it many miles to her home, looking for water and carrying that too on her back. It is a harsh life on the knife-edge of absolute poverty. Yet it is here I turn for an example of a whole and strong and fully human self-image.

The mother of that family has the most powerful sense of joy and happiness, of sheer delight, and her life is blessed by an overriding vision of her self and her family. When she sees one of her children they are immediately swept up into her huge arms and lifted bodily into the universe of her embrace, and upon them falls a shower of kisses. Her constant and healing presence has unleashed the most free and beautiful children one could imagine. Despite the poverty and the disease, the struggles and the harsh climates, there is a wealth of personal self-possession and self–acceptance that is rare. The kindness, patience, humour and laughter that fills the tiny hut should fill every home – human voices, not TV and stereos.

Somehow Western society has managed to lose itself from the primordial freedom and innocence that fill us with simple wonders and joys. Sophistication and attempts to impress each other and score points have destroyed much of our ability to enjoy. As Einstein commented: "We have parties, but we don't celebrate; we eat when we are not hungry, we drink when we are not thirsty; we make noise in case we might hear ourselves."

If I go into a *manyatta* ("home") I am immediately outflanked by a legion of little kids who make a dash for me and haul me through the cow pats into their mummy's home where, amid giggling in the dimly-lit hut, we are given milk, together with all the news, and are surrounded with little friends sitting on lap, back, shoulders and head. In our society, we tend to be less explicit; we often arrive to find everyone plugged into the TV, and the least sign of human life is greeted with a volley of "Shhhh!"

It is true that there is very much love everywhere, but all of us have experienced the conditions and price tags placed upon such offers of love. I'll love you if . . . I'll love you when . . . In a society conditioned to performance and the meeting of stipulations and demands, there is often a condition or a price to my love. Your worth is not in yourself, but in your good looks, your ability to impress people, your obedience to my will, your sense of humour, your doing what is expected of you.

If we have been taught what to do by having love turned on and off, we will associate love with compliance. Wherever love is earned or is at the mercy of another whim, the relationship eventually dies. Such love means that there isn't a two-way sharing. Whether it be close friends, parents and children, man and wife, when communication stops, we feel ever more isolated and alienated.

There are always tragedies that could have been avoided if only . . . The "If only" is usually a reaching out, a getting together, a listening, an understanding.

There was a young teenage girl in high school. She belonged to a staunch family and her father was a leading member of the community. They were strict and religious and they moved in the best social circles. The Young girl

We Stand Alone

lived as many teenagers do, but more and more she felt that she couldn't share her life with her family as they just wouldn't understand where she was coming from.

Then her life became a nightmare. She became pregnant. Whom could she tell, where could she turn? Whatever the situation, the reality was that she felt she could tell no one, and so for nine months she lived in fear and dread. It is a reflection on how close the family was that the girl concealed the pregnancy throughout.

When the time came, it was winter, it was night. She went out to the most secluded place she could find. She was missing for several days. The police eventually found her body huddled up against a wall in the corner of a small shed; beside her was the body of a new-born infant. There had been complications in the delivery. She had died from exposure, internal bleeding and trauma.

The tragedy was real enough and not uncommon. It was more telling that some months after, her young brother committed suicide. If our self-image is to grow, it must be surrounded by understanding and empathy, by humanness and listening.

The example is by no means an exception. Teenage pregnancies in America top 2 million, with half ending in abortion. Of these, 30,000 girls are under fifteen. The peer group places increasing demands on self-images to perform. One article says:

Social workers are unanimous in citing the influence of media, TV and movies in propelling the trend towards precocious sex. Young people are barraged by the message that they must be sexually hip. They don't even buy toothpaste to clean their teeth, they buy it to be sexually attractive.

Time ("Children having Children". 9 December 1985)

All Shall Be Well

In American society, which reflects the rest of Western civilization, 30 per cent of abortions are performed on teenagers. Inflation and unemployment feed an underlying pessimism which is increased by more studies and reports telling us just how deep our problem is. In *Poverty and Family Structure* (Wilson, University of Chicago, 1985), the extent of destructive self-images in America today is shown to be reflected in the scale of the crisis. Murder is the leading cause of death among black males between fifteen and fortyfour. The urban violence seen in most of Europe and America reflects nothing other than a profound distress and loss of self in a society that has little time or inclination to look seriously at its root problems.

While we are filled and coloured by the communal phenomenon around us, there are ways of having a deep and healing self-image despite the negative constraints and demands that are often placed upon us. Self-image can only grow if we slow down long enough to lose the stress and pressure that modern life drags us into. We live in a world where "busy" people are equated with successful people. Busyness is a myth – it means hiding behind a façade of feverish activity and not having the time honestly to face one's life and look where it's going. If we look at the great people of the world, they have always got time for others, always time to listen, to treat you as important and valuable.

Mother Teresa of Calcutta is in demand all over the world to lecture and talk and run her many convents, homes for the dying and services to the destitute. Yet she is always found among the least important and the unwanted. She will sit and talk with them for she has time, simply because she is really busy. Truly active people do not need to perpetuate the illusion of being busy; their lives are filled with what ultimately counts – other people.

Our self-image, if earthbound, becomes an introspective prism of what exists around us. When love is offered, our self-image becomes a realization that we are made in the image of God, we are in his presence, and then we are transformed into a living person.

It is in this fundamental truth of self-presence that is at the core of living spirituality and love: that we discover our own eternity, our own immortality, our own self as God called us to be. In our uncertain search we frequently retreat into the security of the daily things we are used to.

The strange thing about us humans is that we can go through the whole of life in a daze, not knowing why we were here in the first place. We can become so preoccupied and engrossed that we immunize ourselves from everything that disturbs our nest.

We are beings living in time. We are ever conscious of the past and uncertain of the future, often oblivious to the present. We are also, as we will reflect later, guilty of the past and in fear of what might happen in the future. It is these ghosts and uncertainties that destroy the joy of the present. "The man over whom the future has lost its grip, he resembles the birds of the air and the lilies of the field, with no anxieties for tomorrow." (Anthony de Mello, S.J., *The Song of the Bird*).

We need more than ever to be sincerely present to ourselves, to listen to ourselves and examine what lives in our hearts. We have to be honest and unplug ourselves from the radios, TVs and Walkmans, and spend time together with that stranger of our inner selves whom we often forget and do not know.

Presence of self is a phrase very common in both spiritual and psychological study. For our purposes let us restrict its usage to its purest meaning. It is not just self-knowledge or self-understanding, it is a very far reaching awareness and depth. It is a level of self-possession and insights into one's own direction which gives us the ability to see from within, the reality that exists without.

All Shall Be Well

One of the great secrets of the ascended masters in all the great religious traditions, was learning how to live in the gift of the present. Happiness begins by accepting the full import of what my life is here and now. It may be a mess, it may be chaotic, but if I begin to live it I transform uncertainty into hope, and as I deepen in my humanness so too do I become more awakened and alive to my joy.

There are no hidden secrets locked away in far-off monasteries or guarded by ancient monks. There are no magic formulas for acquiring inner happiness or the art of self-awareness. That's what throws many people off the fact that the way of love is threateningly immediate and challenging. It can be started now, in our awareness of everyone and everything around us.

There are many methods and techniques and paths towards inward stillness or self-possession, but whatever the rituals and positions, whatever the procedures and externals, if the method is not born in gentleness and joy, it remains only a method. If it is without love, it remains bereft of life.

An honest, open look at the world is sure to dishearten us and dampen our spirits. But just as we will begin to see the pain and the shame, we will also see all the kindness in our human family. In the course of our efforts among the poor here in Africa, I have encountered racial hatred and bitterness. At times during my travels I met people, quite sincere people, who believe that starvation and famine are natural ways of cutting down the world's population. There are others who seem unmoved by the suffering of the poor and at times this might be discouraging. But there are many other people who rejoice in giving and who extend open arms to all who come their way. Life is never black and white, many of us live somewhere in between these two poles.

Where do I stand in such a world as this? I can only answer

after I have thought about it carefully. I might be sitting on the sidelines cheering the goodies, or I might be digging a bunker to hide from possible missiles that might come my way.

My life might not be doing anyone any harm, I might live by this philosophy: everyone is OK, live and let live. But the real people in a real world are confronted with the present reality that everyone is not OK, and we should examine the cliche more closely and come up with "Live and help others to live" or, as one relief development agency put it: "Live simply so that others might simply live."

True presence of myself means and entails presence to the whole of humanity. Compassion does not discriminate or take account, it has no ideology.

Without a deep conviction or hope in compassion as the way forward, life will seem rather empty, rather frustrating. It can only lead to the inevitable and logical conclusion that we are on our own and it's every man for himself.

CHAPTER THREE

Our Deepest Hope

When we are alone we realize how much we need each other; we realize how much we need other people, and how much we need loving.

The girl peered through the gates of silence. Everything was dark. Fear held her back from going further, doubt veiled her vision, and the cares of tomorrow whispered busily about her.

The gates of solitude bore images of war and blood and the death of splendid things. As they tried to close before her, two angels came to hold them open. One was called Faith and he held open his gate without touching it, but Hope pressed hard with all his strength to open his gate.

They bade the girl walk into the stillness, into the heart of her truth, but it was dark and she was afraid. She was about to turn around and depart feeling defeated, when another came from within the open gates of her heart. His light filled the emptiness and his name was Love.

The deepest and most enduring thirst common to us all is the desire for love and happiness. You and I spend a great part of our lives struggling towards self-fulfilment and joy, while at the same time we are very occupied in the daily responsibilities to our families, our work, the countless little things that absorb our time.

All our emotional scars and mental stress come from the pain of not being fully accepted and cherished

Our Deepest Hope

in ourselves. Anxiety is often related to having to perform and act an acceptable role in order to be admitted into relationships. Ulcers, high blood pressure and heart attacks, insomnia and depression, all stem from trying to do more than we can in a situation that has lost its *humanitas*. If a young mother has a job as a secretary in a company trying to cut expenses, where they start giving her the work of two secretaries and making extra demands on her, she will do all she can to please her employers. In fact, they are causing her to worry, hurry to work and rush home late to her expectant family. Thus, pressure and demands in a business setting lead to anxiety and tension at home. This is what begins to happen in our civilization when we put profit before people, and getting work done before the feelings of those we work with.

We have all, at one time or another, been used, or have experienced someone being unfair to us. We have had embarrassing and hurtful experiences of being humiliated or misunderstood. In family life our small efforts to be courteous and helpful sometimes get crushed or ignored. We know how it feels to be in the wrong and have someone shout at us or frown and walk past. We feel dreadful. We try to be friendly but so often it turns into a strained smile as someone replies curtly and asks what we want. We want to be good, but it's difficult to know a safe place to start. We want to reach out our hand in friendship, but we don't want it bitten off.

If someone humiliates and hurts us, it is difficult to give them a second chance and turn the other cheek. They might just take another swing at us, we are not ready for that kind of abuse. Who needs it?

Because of the distrust that has grown from our experiences, we are very careful whom we welcome. We are selective in our companions, we look suspiciously at those who sit beside us in a bar and start talking to us: "Is he crazy? What's he up to?" we wonder. The city becomes a desert, with groups of friends who are nobody else's friends. As Emily Dickinson, the reclusive poet, once wrote: "The soul selects its own society, then shuts the door."

It is hard for us to know who is for real and who is simply out to get something from us. Is he friendly because I am rich or because I can help him? Does he like me because I am friendly with someone he wants to get to know? What's his angle? We often wonder what people are after. Rarely do we think, what are *we* after, what is *our* angle? Do we offer a carefully measured and compromised relationship, or do we draw our humanity from the bottomless well of authentic love? Do we offer our whole selves, or a tiny fragment from a wounded fort?

What we give and what we want are very different things. When Christ said: "Do to others as you want done unto yourself", he meant also, love others as you would want them to love you. Love is rather a debased and over-used word, which has lost much of its interior meaning and importance. It is necessary to reflect upon the radical implications of what we are searching for and what we desire. We devote much time to hobbies, music, entertainments, work, but most of us rarely dwell too deeply upon the core of life, and the meaning of a lived love. We owe it to ourselves to understand more clearly what it is that drives and motivates and lifts us up.

Genuine love has, by definition, no limitations or demands. It does not suddenly stop in the face of rejection, neither does it dry up over the years to become a habitual acceptance of a stalemate situation. Fake and bogus "love" stops if you don't pay the price for it. Pretended love is at the mercy of our human emotions and mood changes, becoming so unpredictable and demanding that it often degenerates into emotional blackmail and becomes a hurtful not a healing experience, a duty and a pain, not a delight and a celebration.

Authentic love will not require you to dedicate all your freedom to the one being loved, but will open the doors to other paths and other places that need your openness and warmth. In a healthy relationship based on respect, love does not seek to possess or smother anyone, does not need to hang on with both hands to the one loved, but creates a freedom and atmosphere where we can be ourselves. If I cling on to you, you cease to be loved and become a prisoner of my needs.

A young prince was travelling through his country and found, in a village, the most beautiful girl he had ever seen. He brought her back to the palace and planned to marry her. He adored her and bought her everything that money could buy. He was tender and kind and his world revolved around her. His paradise was to be with her every minute of the day, to touch her and look upon her beauty.

But as the weeks went on she began to become ill. After careful and lengthy studies and tests the physicians finally told the prince that the girl was dying.

One day, a weary traveller came to the palace, a priest from the distant monastery on the hill. He told the prince that he could cure the girl and restore her to full life and even make her completely happy, but that the medicine would be very bitter and painful and would cost a great deal.

The prince told the priest that whatever the cost, he would pay, no matter what it took, no matter what the sacrifice.

"My son," the priest said, "the medicine will be painful for you, not for the girl. You have enfolded her in your arms and are blind to all else except the need you have for her. She is grateful and silent, but slowly her life's blood is drawn from her. She is in love with one of your servants. If you love her, let her go, help her and be her friend."

"Let her go . . . ? I never knew . . ." said the prince.

"Because you were deafened by your own voice, blinded by your own passion, warmed by the fires of your own desires and emotions", the priest pointed out gently.

The young prince knelt down and wept. He tore his fine robes and looked up at the priest in despair. He wanted her so much, he could not let her go. He loved her so much, he could not let her die.

Real love is God living inside us. We don't fall in or out of love, it is a constant, it is always there. No matter how frustrated or disillusioned or distracted I may be, no matter how deserted and lost I may feel, or how much I am betrayed, love stands its ground. Even when the ground falls away, love is still there.

If you reject me and do not want my company or my friendship, all I can do is promise you that I believe in you, am there to catch you if you fall, and that if you have nowhere to turn, you are welcome. There is nothing you can do that will destroy the fire of love I have for you. Such love was the love of Jesus Christ. Full, human love is hard for it implies self-sacrifice and putting your needs before mine.

Christian love invites us into the surrender of worldly securities to free ourselves to love in the way Christ loves. It does not mean you must throw away all you have, but it does mean that you must share what you do have, do not close the door, use what you have for the greater good.

Authentic love allows us to lay down our own possessions and comforts. It can only be lived if our life principle is based upon the joy of a living, intimate God who embraces us all. To give when I see nothing that I can gain requires insight into compassion. To care requires the belief that all children, all humanity, all the weak, belong to me – the black and brown, the Hindu and Muslim, the arrogant and the violent, those who shout and fight, those who are meek and quiet.

Ultimately, love is going to mean that I will embrace the whole human experience in my life. I will not edit God, or the diversity of life that he sends my way. Love sometimes means watering the garden so that the flower of another might grow and bloom; it means to generate hope and courage in the garden that God has given us, remembering that he made the great trees and even the tiniest blades of grass. You begin to live in love when you start forgetting yourself, or rather when you are sufficiently happy in yourself, not to need to hold on to your care and troubles. You can help others, not by going on a holy crusade, but by simply being human.

Sometimes we get a bit confused and don't know what we feel. Whatever it may be, it becomes love only when the hand of God makes it so. When the eternal presence breathes upon you, then you begin to love, because it is God loving in you and wherever there is love, there is God. Whenever you love you are praying, and whenever you try to love without looking for anything in return, you make yourself a reflection of what is good and sacred. Whenever you fail and fall far short of love and learn from it and try again, you fulfil the deepest reason of our lives.

The miracle of human life is when we dimly begin to see the vastness and enormity of our humanity, when we touch what is eternal in each other. In a very real sense, for me to love you is for me to see God in you; at the same time to see the real you and accept and rejoice in that discovery. The miracle is when I and thou become we.

If human relationships begin to grow, there are sometimes parts of our characters or something from our past that we feel would endanger the growth or future trust of our bond, so we either hide them or cover them up with lies or defences. Some of our defences are transparent and easily overcome, but others are impregnable walls of fear. A famous film actor had concealed for many years that he had a certain weakness; he was ashamed and never told his wife. Then one day the worst of his fears came true. The Press revealed his secret: that he had been found in his caravan on the filmset with a young man. The Press speculated on forthcoming divorce and had a field day with the scandal.

In a moving biography, the story was retold with all the personal anguish and trauma from the inside. When the Press and others were pouring fires on to the actor's head, his wife returned from abroad in the midst of the sordid, detailed accounts of his crime. She put both hands around his face and said, "I am ashamed, not because of your frailty, but because you doubted my love. I love you and will always love you." Forgiveness was so instant and complete, the richness of her love was so strong, that it wiped away the wound and she helped him surmount the condemnations and judgements. What is important is not to find out the sins and weaknesses of each other, but to forgive, to drop it when we have a stone to throw. When someone stands in front of us and we are in the right whilst they are naked and vulnerable, let it go. It is only when we confront the other in their weakness and forgive that real love is born.

Most of our lives are spent in trying to find such friendships and relationships. Our deepest hope is to be completely loved; we all need help, all want to be lovable, all search for one to love. The search, however, often wavers and crashes on the rocks of failure and defeat. One quarter of marriages in the USA end in separation. Wife and child abuse have become epidemic in many urban environments. Valium is one of the four highest-selling drugs in the world. One in ten American adults has received professional help for mental problems, and the third highest cause of death in the seventeen to twenty-five age group is suicide. One in four British housewives has been on, or is taking, tranquillizers. It would seem that these symptoms reflect a profound discontent, a serious problem in our society that mirrors both the values of that society and the personal visions by which we live.

Psychiatrists don't heal people, love does. Religious practices and rituals do not give us meaning; meaning comes from the living of the Word of God, not its recitation. In the same way, if I tell an unloved person that he is worthwhile, it won't do much good; he has to experience being loved and being wanted before he will be restored. As we discussed in the first two chapters, there is obviously a lot of stress and anxiety in today's world. That anxiety is only lifted when we achieve a degree of inner tranquillity, which only comes from being a self-loving and calm person.

Our desire to be loved, if uneducated and unexamined, remains a deep gut feeling rather than an insight. This basic need to be wanted and loved is exploited all the time. We will follow any possible lead in our efforts to be better-looking, more acceptable and attractive. We are told: "You will be beautiful if you use our shampoo and our cosmetics; without them you won't succeed. You will be sexier if you wear our jeans; you will look like your favourite fantasy figure . . . You will be worth kissing if you have our toothpaste and mouthwash. Wouldn't you like to look like this?" We are sold a notion of what is beautiful, we are educated towards wanting more – more is better, bigger is best. We are not taught the meaning of enough. As Mother Teresa of Calcutta reflects, "We do not know the meaning of enough, we keep looking for more."

Further, we are conditioned to feel that we will not be loved if we are not successful. Success is associated with one's income and social status. We can only free ourselves from such distortions if we learn to think for ourselves as individuals not collectively. In a society that is in need of each personal contribution of ourselves, in a structure that needs a conscience to keep it honest, we have a vital and dynamic role to play.

Unless we strive for goodness, cruelty and intolerance take over. Unless we are always trying to love and trying to make a better world, hate will grow. In the early 30s, as Germany began to build its war machine, the Jewish population saw signs of segregation and propaganda, but they never believed that the mass population of the country would ever let anything serious happen.

The late Dr Jacob Bronowski, like Einstein, spent his life searching and discovering the human condition. He was a questioner and humbly examined our evolution and progression. His series, *The Ascent of Man*, ended with his standing in the pools of Auschwitz where the ashes of millions of Jews and others were scattered. In living memory we had stripped and starved our children, we had shamed them in mindless acts of cruelty, and after numbering them, we sent them to their deaths. There was no room in the plans for these people to live, so the poor, the crippled, the old and the retarded were destroyed along with countless Jews. With tears in his eyes, Bronowski asked the unanswered question: Why? How? When Michael Parkinson interviewed him some time later, Bronowski reflected: "When love is compromised for an ideology or reason, it dies."

When real love exists it does not judge or discriminate, it is not distorted by prejudice or indoctrinated by bigotry. Our society is full of intolerance and outcast minorities. The Palestinians are unwanted in Palestine, the Catholics shoot the Protestants and the Protestants shoot Catholics in retaliation in Northern Ireland. Religious wars shed the blood of the innocent just like any other wars; all war is intrinsically wrong. Whether we discriminate against blacks, homosexuals, political parties or other creeds, or whether we refuse to accept people whom we deem to be below us, intolerance is the same – it's ugly!

In South Africa my black friends would be treated as less than human, without rights, not worthy to walk side by side with whites or live in the same area, they would not be allowed at the same table; they would be considered as a sub-species. Amnesty International say that torture is used in more than a hundred countries worldwide. It has been used not only in the Eastern bloc, but also in England, the USA and many countries that are supposed to uphold freedom and liberty as the right of all. Intolerance is a way of thinking that allows us to remove or repress or condition others as a means of forcing them to change or of removing them from our midst. The meaning of tolerance is an open-minded acceptance and freedom given to those who differ in belief and lifestyle or colour. Love is of its essence tolerant and accepting, not just of the immediately lovable, but of all.

The nature of love causes it to gravitate towards intolerance in an active effort to overcome and heal it, in the same way that Christ met hatred and violence with silence and compassion. Father Teilhard de Chardin, the great thinker and philosopher, believed that the future of man rested in one single realization: that material God and the God of here and now is not real; the only thing that is real is love, and in love lies the future and salvation of the human race. St John of the Cross put it another way: "When we die, we shall be judged only on love."

If a man begins truly to love, then his heart will be big enough to accept everyone; he is filled not only with positive feelings, but with something more potent and universal – the quality of freedom, and the virtue of faith. We hear too much bad news these days, so many hopeless, dead-end stories. But when we love, the good news comes alive in us and like a bush fire it sets light to all the dry and withered life around us.

There are many extraordinary and heroic people. The heroes are not shooting the bad guys or blowing up the enemy, they are not larger than life; they are as weak as you and I. The great people are unseen and silent. They come unannounced into our lives, they give whatever they have and return from whence they came.

There are some rare and wonderful people in your life and much of the good they do is unseen and hidden. One friend of mine was a farmer with little education. He bought a house and filled it with waifs and strays, people who had nowhere to go. He did not advertise his love or ask others to help, he just wanted to give. He visited hospitals and one night got beaten up. He was considered odd and eccentric, but that never deterred him. He got used, conned and dumped on many times; people took him as a fool as he appeared somewhat uncultured with a heavy country accent and no credentials. The charities he helped were countless. He sold his farm and gave away all the money, much of it to our own efforts in Africa and Central America. He continues to welcome any and every one, he continues to be conned and used, but his kindness, resilience and determination are insurmountable. Like Boxer in George Orwell's *Animal Farm*, John keeps adhering to the philosophy: "I must try harder." Certainly his home has been a place of healing to people who had no friends and nowhere else to go. John could never say a bad thing about anyone, only kindness and humour come from him.

Love, like God, shines like the sun; it is not a direct current going from one to another, it is a disposition of the heart. Genuine love is enfolded in the mystery of resurrection and new beginning. It is like the phoenix that rises from its own ashes, new and full of life and power. If God lives in us, we are new and changed each day, we are growing and becoming, learning and discovering ourselves and all around us.

The great mystics and saints reflected and wrote upon the stages and levels of love. From the Hindu mystical writings of the Gita and Upanishads with their steps towards total enlightenment, to the Spiritual Exercises of Ignatius and the Seven Mansions of the Soul by Teresa of Avila, we have one universal starting point. The Little Way of Thérèse of Lisieux is probably the most articulate in its childlike simplicity and forgiveness.

The secret of faith and love is the sacred art of forgiving. All of us have one thing in common, from bishops to pop stars, pensioners to schoolchildren, rich and poor: we are all weak, we are all frail, and we fall many times each day. None of us are as good as we could be, we could all be better, gentler, more merciful. We all remember moments when we caused another person to be very sad or dejected. We all have times when we get angry and make our children cry or frighten a friend. We all know of the times we could have been generous and weren't. The nature of real love can be summarized in a single word, the art of being human can be summarized in the fullness and breadth of that same word: forgiveness.

All the great mystical and spiritual traditions stress this simple gift to each other. All loving begins with a consent to the other and acceptance of their whole being, warts and all, and a joy at and acknowledgement of the beauty of the other. We then celebrate this love in many ways, each one saying, thank you for just being you. If love grows, it does so because we are constantly forgiving each other all the weaknesses, moods and contradictions. We are listening, not just to words, but to expressions, moods, silences; we are reading the whole living situation and are being forgiven all our shortcomings too.

Our lives are for loving, for tolerating each other and

All Shall Be Well

forgiving each other's weak points. Part of love, a very special part of real love, is another often misunderstood human action. It is the act of serving. "Life is to love," said St Bernard to his people, and "Love is to serve."

International rescue teams converged on the disaster zones of Cambodia and took control of the crisis. In many camps there was no sanitation, no food, no medicine, only bomb blasted children, frightened mothers with starved infants, blind men, angry youths, violence. In one such camp there were over 160,000 refugees. The organized relief teams set to work. They divided the camp into sections and set up a hospital that operated round the clock. There was a rumour circulated that some of the refugees had seen an angel, and in fact the angel lived in the camp with the people. The angel was supposed to have a bad leg and talk to God in a strange language, but he loved the people and spoke their language and played with the children.

The workers had little time for such stories as they were occupied getting the camp in order. There were rows and rows of tents where the injured were cared for by a small, hopelessly outnumbered staff. Interpreters were few and often too busy to help out much. One night more casualties arrived in the camp. It was then that the relief doctors had their first chance to see the "angel". At about 2 a.m. he came limping through the aisles of sick people. He stopped at many beds and laughed and joked in fluent Cambodian. He lifted up a child and wiped his nose, and whispered to a blind man huddled in a corner.

He was, of all things, a French Catholic priest; very shy and quiet, but had the most beautiful eyes. He was the light and soul of his people, virtually none of whom were Christian, but that didn't seem to matter too much to him. One night there was a woman covered in burns, her whole front septic from her face to her thighs. She was screaming and shouting. The *abbé* quietly took the instruments from a tired nurse who was unable to approach the woman. He whispered to her and after some twenty minutes began gently to take away the burnt tissues. It took hours. At last he bandaged her, with patience and care and tenderness, talking all the time to her.

He was there to convert no one, to prove nothing; he was there to serve, to love, to witness to the Lord in silent and hidden acts of kindness. He lived in a tiny tent among his people, he kissed the children goodnight, played football with the young men despite his bad leg. He walked among the frightened and the hurt, brought hope and help among them.

Love is the strength to climb out of our trenches and stop worrying about our own security. It is almost impossible to let go of our familiar securities, to take risks and serve those around us. It all depends on the principle that directs our lives. Is it self-protection, self-survival, "me, mine, and keep the head down", or is it "other" and "others"? If we spend our lives afraid to go beyond our own fears and surroundings, we are destined to a safe and secure life, perhaps a comfortable and cosy life, but not a life in which we are ever fully alive or present to the mystery of ourselves. In his book, *Why Am I Afraid to Love?*, John Powell puts it more succinctly. "If we decide to spend our lives seeking the happiness of others, and this is what is implied by love, we shall certainly find our own happiness and fulfilment."

The first schools of Indian mysticism taught a philosophy of self-donation to others, the offering of the mind and soul to all creation, and seeing God reflected in all that he has made. By being gracious and tender to all that God surrounded us with, we accept him as he is. The Sufis taught of a passive awareness and an active caring. Long after the deaths of the great sages, their followers devised formulas and sacred texts and followed them to the letter as the only way to salvation.

Christian tradition also relies upon a living "charity" and kindness, a serving of the weak and those in need. Each of us is called to play a crucial role of service, but there are wounds and problems that inhibit or block the free flow of our gifts. There are things that stop us letting go and loving; there are also things that get in the way of us being loved, that tell us we are not lovable.

All of us have met people who generate a unique magnetism and energy, people whom we feel at ease with. It is easy to love such people. We are healed by them and even when we are far away their memory lifts us up when we feel sad. Deep down in the warmth of our hearts we know that we could go further through such close relationships and share the goodness and kindness that live abundantly in us all. What prevents us from doing so?

We are stopped by uncertainties and fears, doubt and the memories of past experiences. These become obstacles to future growth and happiness, they become ghosts of the past that haunt the future and cloud the present.

There are many complex emotions and responses that prevent us from loving freely. Some involve inferiority feelings and poor selfworth, others are born from disappointments and failed attempts in the past. Our hopes to be loved and to try to love can often be crushed by two common "ghosts" – the fear of criticism, and the anxiety of guilt. To be loved by someone means to be able to entrust them with your weakest self and know that you will never be rejected or analysed by them, only accepted and loved.

The foundation of Christianity lies in the belief that Jesus was the living God, the almighty and absolute power. It was Christ who told us not to condemn or judge, not to criticize each other, or call each other fools. There was a young man recently who committed suicide. In his last note he said that all he had experienced since he left school was condemnation. When his friends found out that he had done a certain wrong, they blamed him and rejected him. He had not experienced any "Yes", so he finally said "No" too, to himself and his useless burnt-out life, which for him had lost any warmth or meaning.

We are all in need of constant affection and affirmation. We are easily hurt, and a kind word, an act of trust, a smile, sometimes makes the difference between a very dark day, and a ray of hope.

In our most private moments when we are alone, or before we sleep, we are momentarily face to face with our real selves. This encounter is often a reluctant and brief experience. The raw truth is often ugly and unwanted; we often don't feel comfortable with what we see.

I feel guilty, guilty of what I have done, of what I should have done, of where I am going. I often don't like my body, my life, the sum total of what God has dumped on me. I have compromised myself to be accepted by people around me and I don't like the result. My guilt is a vague unexpressed anger or stress which is rarely shared. Our lives are projections of how we feel and our faces tell of what we are inside. Our conversation reflects our courage to be ourselves. Guilt is the experience that runs in our subconscious telling us that we have done something wrong, or that we are not doing what we are supposed to do. It reflects our past conditioning and often signifies our unwillingness to forgive ourselves. Guilt is a painful and very common feeling; it hurts and we invariably show it.

We are social animals. We care very much what people think of us and what they say. All too often we prefer to be cautious rather than open about how we feel. It is easier to keep our feelings to ourselves than risk them being laughed at or rejected. There are many people ready to take you down a peg or two, or to deflate your ego. Whatever you do, there will always be someone to volunteer a criticism.

Everyone from St Francis and Gandhi to Martin Luther King is a victim of jealousies, judgements, even persecutions. All goodness exposes itself to being attacked. Little children are told to be quiet and not ask so many questions. Young people are told they cannot change the world and to grow up and be realistic, to stop dreaming, walk the middle path and have some sense. We are told to stick within our limits. All the time we are offered advice. When we are old we are told we are past it, to take it easy. But when Christ came, he said, "Yes, you can change the world. It is OK to dream and live your inner hope into reality. The impossible is possible, miracles take a little longer. Be who you want to be. When St Augustine summarized his life's work, he coined the phrase *Ama et fac quod vis*, Love and do as you like.

People will always pull you down and have a go at you. So what? You are bigger and greater than the mud thrown your way. Live what is inside and don't be afraid. That is the call of Christ, to live what is within your heart.

All of us have been discouraged at one time or another and have felt the pull of others diluting our enthusiasm. I remember when I first ventured into the unknown and decided to go to Africa and the poor countries of the world. There was one very special friend whose voice touched me more than all the dissention and caution. He simply said, "I'm with you all the way. It will be all right and if it goes wrong, I'm always right behind you, I'll always be here." That was enough, and with such love and support anything can be done. He often throws in a lot of concrete, down-to-earth advice in his own humorous and hilarious way. Sometimes we disagree, but his suggestions are made out of sterling love. When we started work on this text at the height of the East African famine, he suggested an honest and human book; not theory, but the joy that comes out of our shared frail human experience.

Our Deepest Hope

When we learn to receive help given in love, we are enriched and we learn. But when we are whipped by cynicism or judgement we remain afraid and injured, unable to let go of the scourging pillar of our own doubt. The only way we overcome the fear of criticism holding us back, is when we experience a loving, supportive encouraging friend; objective, but full of goodness and understanding. Guilt only dies when it is cleansed by forgiveness. The person I am must be free from the stress and anxiety imposed from within and without. I must stop being afraid of being judged and being paralysed by my own guilt.

We must forgive ourselves and have the simplicity of humility to allow others to forgive us. We are weak and in need of mercy and acceptance, we need each other. If we are ever to fulfil our deepest desires and hopes, we should open the doors and see the beauty that lies about us and the readiness of others to accept and support us.

Genuine love is a radically transforming way of life that's free and unconditional. Love is a celebration of all creation, it is a prayer and a sacrifice that tolerates everything. It is hard and demanding. The essence of love is forgiveness, and the nature of love is to serve. Love transforms and deepens, it causes change and a going out of oneself. Love is not always peak experiences of intense, universal dimensions; it is woven into the substance of the simplest acts of everyday life.

We all know the untapped potential that lies within us. We hope some day to free that tide of healing love. We are drawn every day into the relentless search to be more ourselves, more alive. We will live with this hope every day of our lives and no matter how we distract ourselves it will remain with us calling us quietly to find our deepest passion.

Part of our need for love is the need for total love, the love of something else, the drive towards the absolute union. It is a dream that dares to hope in a perpetual intimacy, that there is a God, a Father, who loves us utterly and fully beyond our wildest imaginings.

CHAPTER FOUR

In Search of the Sacred

Somewhere in our human experience there is a suspicion no matter how vague, that there is something else happening. We are caught up with what is going on in the visible world, but are constantly drawn by an awareness of another existence, a different reality. No matter how removed this reality might be, we are frequently drawn to it. Most people only have enough time to notice this deeper part in the smile of a child, or the rare instant of affinity with nature, or in the moment of death or birth. A whisper of the mystery occasionally causes us to wonder.

This illusive part of our lives has been given many labels. Some philosophers call it the "reflective subconscious", others, "auto-suggestive illusionary fantasy". For some it is simply an "I don't know" part of life. For others it may be termed spirituality. Most spiritual traditions are embodied in infrastructures called religions, some of which are intricately evolved and organized into institutions; others are small communities who follow a simple, shared way of life in an attempt to develop their spiritual lives.

Some religions have universities and experts in many fields. Others have little or no knowledge of academic expertise. Either way, spirituality remains a strange, unknowable mystery beyond us all, and the essential truth may be summarized in a single word: loving. There are no professors of loving, no specialists in kindness, there are only kind, loving people.

One of the problems of the twentieth century has been

All Shall Be Well

a tremendous desertion from institutionalized religions on the grounds that they tend to be above the heads of ordinary people and talk down to them. We need the humility to say we don't know, that I, like you, am searching and trying to be better. Let us look to each other and maybe we will find a few answers together.

The questions themselves are pretty foreboding. Why suffering? Why wars? Why tiny infants starving and full of diseases? The problems of evil and pain, of loneliness and inequality. Where do we even begin to dig out the answers? The journey of discovery is what life is about. The time when our behaviour begins to become transformed into a living celebration is the time when we see the first signs of a true spirituality.

As we said in the previous chapter, we are in search of love, we are in search of each other. But ultimately all these things mean we are in search of the origin and source of love: God.

The great mystics ascended to extraordinary levels of intimacy and intense union with God. Their experiences came from the spirit of love within and lifted them into unimaginable ecstasies and states of incommunicable knowledge. While such phenomena of the direct experience of God can be very encouraging, most of us do not experience God in such dramatic terms. For most of us he is an unpredictable, invisible enigma, who never seems to be there when we call.

Many of us find that the central pillar of spirituality is prayer, that thing we do before exams, in times of illness and panic. Prayer is often an eleventh-hour attempt at rescuing a situation. For most people, prayer is an uphill struggle against distractions and immediate demands and preoccupations.

Whatever we call God, or ask of him, he always seems to be silent or too busy to listen. Yet he is never far away, but

In Search of the Sacred

can be found in the smile of a friend, the giggle of a child, the tranquillity of the ocean. When face to face with the majesty of his creation, we often feel the presence of the creator.

One day, the beggar Saint Francis of Assisi sat for hours upon the hillside. In the evening, one of the young monks was sent to look for him. "What are you doing, Brother Francis? The monks are about to greet the Bishop who comes this evening!"

Francis looked down. "Little brother," he said. "I am listening to the voice of God."

"But I hear nothing, only the wind and the stream and the birds," replied the young man.

"Listen again, little one," said Francis, "and they will awaken something in your heart that is beyond all knowledge." The young man lay on the grass and closed his eyes. After a long time Francis asked the monk, "Did you hear the birds singing?"

"Yes."

"Well, now you know all the secrets hidden in all the great books of the library, and the longing of the saints." The young man felt his deeper secret which could not be spoken and which knew no thoughts.

Religion is only true religion when it comes from inside you, when it comes from the most personal part of you and is offered up freely and completely. If one knows the Scriptures and keeps the laws and wears the robes of the holy man, if one preaches and teaches from the doctrines and moral laws, this may be very good. But if I give one single moment from my heart and look up and cry "Help!" then this is prayer. This is the true rock of religion.

St Thomas Aquinas was the most influential and powerful theologian in Christendom for 700 years. His works inspired Christian thought and provided the most complete summary of Christian teaching, influencing even Vatican II.

Towards the end of his long and fruitful life, he suddenly stopped writing. His sudden decision prompted much speculation and many noted scholars appealed to him. Finally he confided to a close friend why he had decided to stop. One night while he was praying he had passed from a very lonely hour into what he could only call an experience of the divine, a moment of intimate closeness with God. After this, all he had ever written seemed so poor, and was "straw compared to that moment of love". Since then he had felt no desire to write. His union was enough.

One of the biggest stumbling blocks in searching for a loving God is often those very institutions that purport to be teaching about God. Often, people reject God because of the hypocrisy and attitudes they see reflected in those who hold themselves up as examples of religious practice. This is nothing new. Pharisees, many of whom are sincere, can be off-putting to those honestly seeking a living witness and a living God.

We must not judge religion by the frailty of its followers, but rather by the depths of love and mercy that it reflects and invites us to share. We must not expect men to be divine or have angelic purity, nor must we expect the structural ideologies to reflect the intimate, passionate love that God gives to us in the stillness of our hearts. The problem often starts in the confusion between the accidentals and exteriors of a church and the interior essentials of spiritual life, common to all loving and prayerful men regardless of creed or denomination.

If you have ever sat down with a friend who claims to be an atheist, you will have found that they are usually of two types. The first may often be a very angry person who will

In Search of the Sacred

disagree with everything you say. In this situation there is little point in dialogue as the person is perhaps not yet ready to grow. The second kind of atheist is often a very genuine and insightful person who is full of questions and receptive to honest answers, not platitudes or pretentious piety. They cannot reconcile certain trends in Church thinking with the state of the world, they revolt against hypocrisy and often stress social action and radical change. Their complaints are often similar to those of Luther and liberation theology, and they are often people who in their own lives are very generous and searching. In reality they may be more sincere in their search than many of the outwardly acceptable and hard-line believers.

In the age of cults, new religions and factions, alternative spiritualities and lifestyles, it is easy for people to get misled by bogus ideologies that promise self-enlightenment, self-discovery and self-elation. On the other side of the fence there are those who use stark and formal formulae bound by traditional ritual to address a staunch, sometimes vengeful God.

Religion should, like Christ, live where the common man lives, not theorize over his head. If religious ideals hurt or dehumanize us they become unjust and a subtle form of persecution. God, in his understanding, changed the Word into flesh and blood, not into theological propositions. He came to where most of us live, to heal the rifts and conflicts, to turn tensions and divisions into a healing and human wholeness. If we hide behind the practices and formulae of religions we can often miss the point of it all. The point is joy, the proof is how kind and happy we are in our lives.

We must remember that the disciples walked with the living God and looked upon his face, yet even so they were afraid and uncertain. They were sincere, but they were, like us, full of conflict and paradox. They had seen a blurred and distant vision of a true God. The Pharisees had little

All Shall Be Well

patience with such ambiguity and held rigidly to their clear and distinct vision of a harsh, legal God.

A lot of harm has been done in the past by men zealously preaching their own versions of God. Wars have been waged in the name of a God of peace, and tears have been wept from the cruelties of men preaching a God of joy. Throughout the Middle Ages an obsessive search for an emasculated purity dominated religious writing and left deep emotional scars on generations. Even today there is a great need for a more human acceptance of sexuality and affection, and a compassionate and frank look at our dual moral codes. We need to grow in our understanding of touch, of tenderness, of shared affection and expression. We have buried much of what is beautiful, partly from distorted religious taboos and rigid rules that have been applied universally.

Of late there have been great changes, healing developments, all over the world – people are coming together and searching, trying, praying, questioning, helping. Church, whatever banner or label may be on it, is essentially this dynamic struggle to love and live. It lies in the struggle of human life and human pain. Religion, the binding back of life to its centre, is here, in the growth of God in our lives here and now.

In the past God has been portrayed as someone remote from humanity, and such a God chilled the hearts of real people. Saints are not plaster statues staring angelically upwards brandishing crucifixes and flowers. They are and always were very real and weak people who dared to live the impossible into reality. They are people who cry and tremble, who make mistakes and get on people's nerves. Saints have fears and passions and the same sins we all share. The difference is that they accept and embrace the mystical love offered to them in the miracle of life, they respond to it in a powerful and beautiful way, they become fully alive and touch the deepest cord of mankind in their happiness and love. A saint is a person who lives in gentle love and union with God and celebrates God in the highest and greatest of all prayers, the prayer of total trust and sincere service.

The great Russian writer, Tolstoy, recounted an old legend common in the Volga district, in one of his short stories, *The Three Hermits*.

A Bishop's ship, was carrying pilgrims from Archangel to the Soiovetsk Monastery to visit the shrines of that place. One of the seafarers was telling some of the pilgrims of three holy men who lived on an island near to where the ship was passing. The Bishop asked if they were Christians, and of what Order. The seafarer grew silent and unsure, and told the Bishop that the three hermits were very simple men who did not know of orthodoxy or rule. The Bishop determined to see these hermits for himself and ordered the Captain to take them to the island.

After some time, the Bishop landed with a small party of priests and found the three old men tending a small garden. He questioned the men and found that they were illiterate and knew nothing of church feasts or services or Scriptures. They had never heard of doctrine. The Bishop was aghast and spent the afternoon laboriously teaching the three old men the Lord's Prayer. The Bishop had been shocked by the primitive way in which they had been praying, for they had told him: "We lift our eyes in heaven. We say, 'We are three, you are three, have mercy on us'."

The Bishop left the island late that evening pleased that he had at least corrected a serious heresy and blasphemy. As he left, the three old men bowed humbly towards the Bishop and thanked him profusely for his teaching and the new prayer.

Not long after, the Bishop's ship was returning to his city and was passing some thirty miles from the island. The seaman in the crow's nest called to the Captain of an

All Shall Be Well

approaching ship, and sure enough there was a light in the distance that seemed to grow as it moved over the turbulent sea towards them. It moved so fast that many of the crew grew afraid. The Bishop stared with awe as he saw the three old men, hands joined, illuminated in a strange light and running towards the ship over the water. They greeted him joyfully and bowed humbly to the Lord Bishop. "What is it you want?" asked the Bishop, trembling.

"Holy Bishop – we sorry – we forgot beautiful prayer you teached us. We mixed up words and cannot remember. Please teach us how to pray again."

The Bishop looked upon them, as the Spirit of God shone all around them. He bowed his head humbly and said, "Children of God, go home, and each time you pray, say 'We are three, you are three, have mercy on us'."

God looks into our hearts as we live our daily lives. "He knows what you need before you say it, so when you pray don't pretend or be seen by others, go into your inner room and in secret pray to your Father who is there in the secret place, and your Father who dwells there will answer you (Matthew 6:6).

This essential core of faith and love is hoped for and searched for in many ways by all of us. It must not be confused with the accidentals and exteriors of religious traditions. No matter how centre-stage liturgy and clergy, theology and philosophy, appear to be, they are merely there to help and to cultivate an understanding and a way of living. When these exterior acts become more important than love and charity, religion becomes an empty autocracy of law and form. It is given life only when its followers live the redemption and the Passion and the joy of a dynamic and celebrating Father.

From a theological or theoretic viewpoint, the church as a formal entity must be divided into carefully defined parts.

In Search of the Sacred

Some of these enter into metaphysical and ontological areas, others into very concrete moral issues and temporal realities. For the sake of our present concern let us be content to say that the Church is basically composed of four interlinked component parts, each valid and essential to its fabric and function.

This simple formula is applicable to any of the great religions, Islam, Hinduism, Christianity, Judaism, Buddhism and their countless denominations. It also applies to varying degrees, to loosely formed sects and cults and even to individuals who have themselves decided upon a non-institutional and personalized relationship with God.

1. Creed

A creed is what I profess to believe in. All of us believe in something no matter how cosmic or vague. Some of us express belief by adopting an articled statement listing all those things we hold as true. Others, perhaps most of us, are less clear where our trust and belief lie. At the same time most of us hold and trust that there is some power greater than ourselves. We search, and in our search we do profess a conviction that there is a something. The creed of Islam is an uncompromising and absolute tenet that Allah is One God and Mohammed is his only prophet and that none is to be worshipped but him; it is a categorical statement not open to interpretation. The Catholic faith maintains a similar line in its one true Church, though since the Second Vatican Council it has modified its more conservative stance. Such expressions of absolute truth have tended to unease modern men who have moved in thinking towards a more universal creed of shared humanity, a real ecumenism, a shared common destiny and spiritual heritage based upon love and trust and compassion.

A creed, therefore, is what we profess, not necessarily what we always put into practice. It is more the ideal and the essence of one's faith as opposed to the daily policies by which we live.

2. Code

Most religions have some form of code by which the faithful are expected to abide. These embrace the doctrines, scriptures and uniform practices guiding the functions and structures of religions. The codes embrace teachings on moral and religious matters. For some they lie in canonical laws and ecclesiastical directives and pastorals; for others they are a more subjective code of morality, coloured both by one's previous conditioning and experience and one's personal judgement.

3. Cult

The cult of a religion is perhaps most easily summarized by its exterior forms, its labels and accidentals, those external practices and symbols that identify the followers as members. In recent times the phrase has been associated with obscure neo-Hindu cults and sects who adopt strange habits and do things alien to Western culture. Those have, in the last few years, been replaced by more balanced movements less reliant on exterior signs of devotion and show. The cult of religion is usually drawn from its history. The outward displays of religious fervour, the incantations and liturgies, the ceremonial magisterium, all these are part of our upbringing, they embrace a communal worship through which we learn and adopt the code of behaviour of that religion and communally profess the adopted creed of that Church.

Many people, especially young people, have rejected the creed, code and cult of institutional structures and religions with the accusation that such things are to them hypocritical and empty. They feel very angry about the

In Search of the Sacred

accidentals, the showing off, the Sunday act, the façade of the saved and the godliness of the ungodly. One very common attack is a personal reaction to a minister or priest. "When I was sick, he never came to see me. He visits the fancy suburb but has never come to our flats." People react very strongly to example and feel very deeply, and we must admit that there have been and are shortcomings in our churches; there is pettiness and introspection. But we must never forget that something pure is unstained, even if offered to us by a sullied hand. Gold is still gold no matter who holds it. The truth is always the truth no matter how we try to twist and bend it.

In thinking of religion we must remember that we are still all weak, all sinners, all far short of the mark, and instead of rejecting God because of the frailties of his priests and ministers, we should accept and embrace him even more in our own frailties. We should accept and see God, not through the creeds or the practice or the external functions around us, but for the fourth and most vital element of all religion, its breath and its fire.

4. Spirit

The most important part of religion is the spirit, the love and fire in a man's heart placed there by a living and active relationship of trust and friendship. The essence of religion is how I love my God in the privacy of my heart and the gift of my neighbour.

All things are relative and will pass away, only love remains. The greatest of all mystics, St John of the Cross, summed it up in the words: "In the last, in the final moments, we shall be judged on love." Love is the Spirit of God living and acting in each little deed of today. The meaning of religion is in where the word comes from – the returning back, the binding back, back to the centre of life and the axis of our hearts, back to the source of love and life which is the Spirit and joy of an intimate and loving God who cherishes and rejoices in his creation.

If one were to summarize every book of sacred teaching and every inspired writing from the beginning, then draw together every Saint and sage to produce a formula, one might end up with a poor attempt at the Sermon on the Mount. For a brief summary one might turn to Julian of Norwich: "It is love."

The depth and meaning of religion is the spirit that lives in the heart of its members. We can hang on to all the pieties and customs, adhere to all the traditions, but they are somehow empty if they are not lived. At Christmas, we light a candle at our window as a sign of welcome, that Christ is welcome into our homes. To Dorothy Day, who worked tirelessly in the inner city of New York among the poor, the desperate, the hurt, the candle meant welcoming Christ no matter how he walked into her life. It meant that there was always room at her table, always room in her home, plenty of room to make a better world. The Spirit of God is the essential core and axis from which all faith takes its strength. It is the spark that allows us to serve even when we are misunderstood and our motives questioned.

The Spirit of God is incarnate in his children as an unending act of love which is cherished and abides. Only those who see the invisible can do the impossible, only those who are touched by the joy of a loving gentle Lord can forgive and walk all the way. Only I can accept for myself the risk of such intimacy, only I can make the vision real, only I can reach out and respond to the invitation. It is and will always be the ultimate risk, the greatest challenge, to open one's heart to the hidden and touch something of his presence and his will, that we become one with him, one in love, one in the spirit of life, equal and whole, not unequal and separate.

It is easy to fool ourselves that on the surface we are doing the best we can, we are OK, but the more we question and examine our lives the more we realize that we could become better. If we stop growing we start dying; we are alive only in as far as we are receptive and alert and ready to make changes in an open and frank way. If we begin to see the beauty inside us and the power of love ready to come out, we will be willing to change some of the defences and walls that we have built, to open up that love and offer it in frail and uncertain hands to those around us.

We were created in God's image, yet we relentlessly search for a God who will manage to fit our image, a God who will find a slot in our lifestyle, who will agree to let us hold on to the things we depend on. We talk to him half-heartedly just in case he might by chance be there. The honest search leads us towards a different language, a strange language which is hard and difficult to learn in a modern world. It is the language of the saints. It was spoken before creation and is the deepest language of the human heart, the mystery of inner silence.

Spirituality is that something that brings forth in us an inner transformation, a wordless insight and wisdom. The acid test of a living search for God, of a sincere spirituality, is not how prayerful we are, nor how hard we work, nor so much what we profess, but what we are like to live with and be with. The bottom line is how we treat each other, not just family and friends, but strangers and those we consider aggressive and irritating.

Honesty means not looking for God for my own peace of mind and salvation. It means that I offer him all human need and sorrow in my silence. I take with me my human family and call them mine. I walk into the uncertainty of the abyss not obsessed with or made helpless by the plight of humanity, but confident that our Father will bring new hope, new ways, and radical progress through his children for a more loving world.

It is dishonest to rely on the experience of others in your

relationship with God, or to abdicate your shared responsibility to the weak among us by saying it's not your job. We were all called to love personally. No one can pray your prayer or give the secret of your heart, just as no one can kiss on your behalf. Your act of trust and love comes from you, it enfolds and lifts up your senses and experience, it is the harmony of all your emotions and the elation of your experience. It is felt and known by only you and the Beloved. Your act of love is your most private gift in which you lay yourself naked in trust and integrity. So too in prayer, the whole self is offered and given in an act of trust and surrender to be accepted and healed in the arms of God.

No one can find your meaning for you or walk into your silence. It must be done by you and can only be done if, in your heart, you believe you will not be left alone, and that through the darkness and silence there will come a wholeness and presence. We often run from such times of silence, we often panic at the thought of long, lonely stillness where we confront only our imaginings and fears. The ordinary mind boggles before the enormity of the proposition that God would bother to move in me and touch my boring ordinariness with himself. Most people are so overwhelmed by such lofty thoughts that they leave them to saints or theorists, to others better equipped for closeness to God.

St Bernard of Clairvaux said that joy was the infallible sign of the presence of God. Most of his sermons were on love and kindness, and his favourite examples were taken from John, the disciple whom Jesus loved, and from the Song of Solomon.

Bernard, like so many of the great mystics, tried to free God from the limitations and concepts that men placed on him. Closeness to the breath of life came not by earth-shattering ecstasies, but through the opening of the mind to

In Search of the Sacred

see the ordinary things, the most mundane daily chores, as part of the gift of life, and in that gift, the mystery and pattern of all his creation dancing around us. The search begins in the routine of our lives, not in deserts or great monasteries, but in the dwelling place of the heart. Bernard's contemplative life could be summarized in his phrase: "To live is to love, to love is to serve." Through internal calm and peace, all one's actions would find a harmony and the life of the contemplative would be a call of sanity in a raging world, his home a place of rest and refuge, the doors always open to those in need. To Bernard, as to Benedict before him, the stranger, the visitor, all men, were the Christ, to be respected and loved and cared for; the care of the stranger, the welcome of the leper, was to be a welcome of Christ.

There are many great writings and paths that have been given us by the good men of all faiths. Like Bernard and Benedict, many of the great spiritual paths were disciplined and formed into schools of thought which evolved into systematic ideas. There was often stagnation and dilution of their original vision, so, as history moves on, there are others who express the same vision in other ways, some more academically than others. All are concerned with the same search for God, for the sacred, and how to live the divine in the fragile reality in which we live and struggle.

Many of the great spiritual writers wrote in a devotional, somewhat archaic style which switches off the modern reader, but there are notable exceptions worth mentioning. Their simple advice is as relevant in the great cities of today as in the stark crisis areas of the world.

There was an illiterate lay-brother called Lawrence who looked after the menial tasks in a small Carmelite monastery in the sixteenth century. It was a time of violence, wars, plague and great unrest. In the midst of the chaos something about this shy little man set fire to the hearts of all who met him, and his strange joy attracted people from all over to seek his advice and the secret of his happiness.

He dictated a very short journey of a soul, called *The Practice of the Presence of God*. This humble writing reflected the essence of human happiness, and his unschooled and simple mind spoke in human terms without special language or explanations. In it, Lawrence said that by trusting the unseen, suspicions and criticisms began to die, and because everything became so exciting and wonderful, one remained never afraid, always calm, always possessed by patience. No one's anger or petulance could fluster you because the presence inside was greater and bigger than the problems on the surface of life. Lawrence realized he was like a little child, helpless to change anything, but by trusting in his gentle Lord and calling on his power, anything could be done.

So the search for God starts with little things, it begins gradually by becoming aware of life and of the countless gifts around us. But what about those of us who don't have time for a patient discovery of their own mystery? There are many among us. Where is the sacred? Where is hope for an AIDS victim or a young parent told that they are terminally ill? Where do they turn, who can they hold on to in their anxiety?

When the material God is gone and there is no more need for possessions or bank accounts, no more role-plays or pretences left, we stand alone and feel desolate and abandoned. Those who deal with the dying can do it in two ways: clinically, with a professional detachment; or, like Mother Teresa and Jean Vanier and countless unnamed nurses and doctors, they can be simply human, giving the only thing left to give – presence, and through that human presence, there is a greater presence.

From the darkness there is a whisper: "Be happy little one, it is I, do not fear any more" (see Matthew 14:27). He is pure and utter joy and has "gathered the broken and the

In Search of the Sacred

hurt, those who have been driven out and those who are afflicted. And he will bring the outcast into His Paradise and there he will love them always" (Micah 4:6–7).

The search for God often only begins when we are face to face with death, or when someone we love very much is taken from us. Like Job we scream into the abyss: "Why? You are a cruel God. Why have you taken him from me? He was all I had. Why?" A friend of mine turned to me one day and told me that God did not exist. His reasoning was based on the agonies and private torments he had seen, the cesspool of an inner city with so much hate and bitterness. What kind of God could let that happen? A frightened kid raped by a gang, a student getting her brains blown out for a few dollars. His was the same cry that has echoed the four corners of the torn earth from the beginning: "Out of the depths I have cried to you, O Lord . . . and you did not answer. You did not hold me when I needed you . . ." We pray at our best in times of anger or loss, during moments of despair or betrayal.

At a great age, St Teresa of Avila went on a mission of mercy. She travelled over treacherous roads to Granada and in dead of winter fell badly into an ice pool full of mud. The aged foundress of the Carmelite Reform stood up, black with mud, shaking her fist. "No wonder you have so few friends. What else do you want now?" Teresa believed in open and straight words, even to God. Perhaps because of this, she reached such depths in prayer. When in dialogue with God, externals did not matter, her mind surrendered and was suspended within the timeless ambience of God.

When we confront an impossible task, or have to share in the dying of someone close to us, we feel very small and helpless and we search the darkness for an answer. Much of the anxiety lies in the doubt we have in another world, in the risk that the one we love might just fall into a nothingness oblivion and be no more. There comes a point when we must let go and let God be God. When the sum of human life is ended, a dying man does not need the diagnosis of experts or consultation, but the love and understanding of another human being. "Lord death is ugly and mean, where has he gone to?" "He has made everything beautiful and complete in its own time. He has planted eternity in their hearts ... and the joy of men is to do good all their lives ... and they will all return to him" (Ecclesiastes 3:11, 12, 20).

Our yearning for God fluctuates as we feel we need him. Persecuted and hated peoples turn to him in times of need. We turn to him when in pain or trouble, yet a life of closeness to God should become an intimacy born of daily trust, and the prayer of our living actions should be a conscious act of love.

We look for God in many places, we call him by many names. But often we look for him to do our will and are not prepared to accept the radical and transforming gift that is *his* will. We are forever in search of the holy and eternal, but when we find it we recoil and retreat because it is a great cliff and below there is an uncertain, bottomless drop and a voice whispers, "Jump!"

The world is dislocated from itself and we are dislocated from the celebration that life is supposed to be. We are filled with fear and confusion. While we need to be loved by each other, we are also in need of the love of our Lord, our creator. We all want to be good, we all need to be safe in his arms. We will never be fully ourselves without his Spirit living inside us.

To this end we spend our lives trying to know whole and dynamic love. We were given arms to embrace each other, eyes to look upon the beauty of each other, backs to carry each other and mouths to smile. We were given ears to listen, and hearts to love, and minds to understand. But above all we were given tears to cleanse, and spirits to unite us together for ever.

In Search of the Sacred

So where do we find God, this strange, hidden enigma? He comes in many disguises, in the leper, in the unwanted, in the dull and ignorant. He comes to our front door as a beggar. It is easy to have sympathy for the Christ of the hungry when he is thousands of miles away, but when he stands on our own doorstep it is harder to accept and embrace him.

He comes to us and he will come again. "He came among them, and they knew him not, and they did not receive him" (John 1:1). The discovery and search for God is, more accurately, a realization of one's inner self and a recognition and acceptance of the living God, alive and brooding and dwelling within your soul.

CHAPTER FIVE

Christ, the Gentle Lover

For many of us, our search takes us into the life of a man we know very little about – a vagabond itinerant preacher, a social reject, accused of revolution. He was born without any place to lay his head, was persecuted and fled to Egypt as a refugee. This simple tradesman was either a fraud, an outrageous hoax, or, as the basis of Christianity, he was the Son of the living God, the Creator of the universe, the origin and destiny of mankind.

If we see Jesus merely as a holy man with a good message, full of good life principles and precepts, we have missed the point. The whole meaning of Christ was that in and with him, there was a resurrection, a dawn of the spirit, a new beginning, a transformation of everything.

The question still haunts us: if Jesus really was God, why didn't he make his presence felt more, why didn't he wipe out the Pharisees and the Romans, or at least stop them from getting in his way? Why didn't he stop the torture of innocent Jews and the execution of John the Baptist? Why bother coming as a carpenter? Why not come as a Roman senator or in some other official role? Why come at all . . . ?

In the classic epic, *The Brothers Karamazov*, Dostoevsky tells the story of the Grand Inquisitor. The figure of Christ reflects you and me, the misunderstood, and at times it reflects those around us, those we see and those we do not wish to see.

It was the middle of the fifteenth century, the height of the Spanish Inquisition. Christ was seen on the steps of the cathedral. He was healing the cripples and giving sight to

Christ, the Gentle Lover

the blind and raising the dead. He restored the body of a man who died from the Black Death, and a great throng gathered in the Cathedral Square.

A solemn procession arrived; cowled monks and armoured soldiers preceded the aged Cardinal who had been appointed by God through Philip of Spain to be Grand Inquisitor of the Holy Inquisition. The guards seized the healer and caried him through the doors of the cathedral and out the back, through the streets and into the palace of the Cardinal. In the dungeons below, he was beaten and tortured, stripped and interrogated. His silence angered impatient monks who struck him again. At last his bruised and battered body was hurled into a dark dungeon.

The Cardinal was old, his face grey and wizened, wrinkled and lean, his pursed lips bloodless and tight. He bore life as a burden, without emotion. The earth was a place of sin and a valley of tears. He could not sleep that night and, after midnight, the gaolers opened the heavy door of the cell. The Inquisitor stared at the bruised and stained face of his Lord.

After some time, the old Cardinal began: "Why have you come? Why have you come again to haunt us? We have corrected your work and made your words real for these people. You asked from them too much more than they could ever give, you gave us an impossible burden. You who are God do not know how weak your creatures are. Your only answer to their plagues and wars, their cruelties and sufferings, is to stand up and tell them they should love each other." The Inquisitor spoke long into the night. "Where is your love for us? Look what you have done to us," and the tall figure pointed towards the damp stone wall and out to the humming city beyond.

His cold face, severe and dark, glared at the prisoner before him. "Just as they praised you today, so they shall heap faggots on to the flame tomorrow, and those you healed shall cry 'Heretic!' You were never meant for such a

All Shall Be Well

world as this. You are innocent and naïve to think that men could follow such a pure way. Your hand could stay the sword, but the children are slaughtered. Your hands are as red as mine."

All the while, the old man was waiting for some answer, some reaction from Christ. He wanted Christ to cast him down or shout or rage, yet all he did was stand looking into the old man's dark eyes.

"What do you say, now that I condemn you?"

But the naked man did not speak. He moved a few steps towards the old man who stumbled backwards. The Cardinal put up a jewelled hand to hold back the guards, his eyes staring in fear at the bloodied figure before him, and he trembled. Christ gently placed a hand upon the old man's shoulder and then slowly kissed him on the lips.

In the eternity of silence that followed, the old man was broken and ashamed. He was torn and transfixed. He opened the small door which led into the dark alley of the city. "Go, and come no more," he said, and the figure passed by him and disappeared into the darkness. The old man stared into the night which hid the tears that fell upon his grey face.

No matter how bad we are, no matter how full of sin, no matter how deep our betrayal and denial, or how often we hurt him, his arms are open to catch us when we fall and to lift us up to his embrace.

We all feel every now and then that people are putting us down and criticizing us, picking holes in the least things we do. Some people do it for spite, others because of jealousy, others for "our own good". Whatever the reason, it causes pain which we don't need. No matter who judges us or rejects us, he, the Christ, is always there at our side. If we see him and allow him to come into our lives, we become healed and unafraid.

All of us, young and old, powerful and weak, rich and

Christ, the Gentle Lover

poor, share one thing in common: we could all be better, more loving human beings. We have more to give and for many reasons much of our inner potential remains unused. In short, we are all sinners, we all fall a bit short of the mark. Most of us aren't bad people, we are good; but sin isn't what bad people do, it's what good people don't do. As Paul puts it, "He is light, you and I are only flesh and we often fall. We don't understand what we are doing. The good we want to do, we don't do, and those things we don't want to do, we do" (see Romans 7:14).

We hurt each other and disappoint friends, we shout at a child and frighten him, we say things in anger that we don't really mean, and in our work we can be unthinking and demanding of those under us. None of us are as good as we could be, we all need help and all need to be encouraged and strengthened and backed up. Our sins are not so much premeditated acts of cruelty, as little moods of pettiness and selfishness, lack of common sense and understanding, lack of tact and patience. We might not batter our wife to death, but we might come home tired and sit in front of the TV ignoring all her efforts to make the place lovely, and her painstaking care over the cooking might be discarded in a grunt. Grumbling or absence of feeling can make or crush a person's day.

Our little sins are our attempted expediences of the moment, shortcuts to immediate contentment. Sins are those things done without love. They are not so much the negative things, but the absence of positive things, the absence of love. Sin is when we live without compassion and kindness. Christ never sinned because he *was* compassion.

Humanity comes the more we learn how to give. There is heroic caring and giving all around us, unselfishness and greatness. If you have ever seen the selfless care given by the parents of a handicapped child, you can see that their devotion and infinite patience is born from a determined and boundless love. This is true of many families, but the sacrifice required by families of the severely handicapped, the unseen everyday acts of love and affection, remain a poignant example of unrestricted giving. In the extreme poverty of Africa where such mothers do not even have tomorrow's food, the giving becomes even more remarkable. These people give with joy and delight, oblivious of their own circumstances. "Through the hands of such as these, God speaks, and from behind their eyes he smiles upon the earth," says Kahlil Gibran in *The Prophet*.

In an interview, Malcolm Muggeridge once asked Cardinal Heenan what he considered to be the greatest theological mystery of all. Some expected the answer to be the incarnation, others, the resurrection, others, eternity. Yet the mystery that touched him most deeply was none of these. It was that the Author of life, the absolute God, not only knew of him, but loved him as though there was no one else in the world, and that his name was carved upon the hand of God. The mystery that he was loved so much, wanted so much, was for him the most mind-boggling and inexplicable of all.

There have been very great men, holy men, even divinely inspired men and women. What was so completely different in the life of Jesus Christ? The answer almost certainly lies in his forgiveness, his acceptance, his mercy. He identified himself with the lost, the rejected, those deemed as unfit and unworthy. He was among the prostitutes and sick, the tax collectors and thieves. These, who were the most unwanted and despised, first saw the quality and power of his mercy and forgiveness.

It takes more than greatness to forgive mindless violence or treason. Even Peter, who had denied his Lord, tasted mercy for we are told that "The Lord looked straight at Peter, and Peter went outside and wept bitterly."

No matter what we have done with our past, He is there.

Christ, the Gentle Lover

We are afraid of looking upon him and being rejected or reproached, of being told he no longer wants us any more because we have hurt him and betrayed his trust. All of us to some extent are guilty of compromising ourselves, of opting for the practical and the expedient. We have sacrificed much of our deeper selves on the altar of social norms and we have buried much of our vision for fear others will run away from us.

When Christ looked upon the face of Pilate or Peter or the adulterous woman or the rich young man or Mary Magdalene, they saw in his eyes the same thing that the soldiers who scourged him saw – that there was no accusation, no condemnation, no hatred or vengeance or anger. And when we too dare to look into his eyes we see no demand. He is saying, "I will not hurt you, I do not condemn you. I love you, nothing you can do will make me reject you." Only God can love like this, only he can us forgive so utterly.

One of the most beautiful and mystical expressions of God's love is in his words to Hosea: "It was I who took them up in my arms, yet they did not know that it was I who healed them. With human hands I led them with the touch of my love" (Hosea 11:3).

Christ simply came and lived among us. He stated his truth quietly and promised us fidelity and that he would be at our side always. He offered hope in a hopeless world, sanity in the face of madness. He made sense of pain and spoke of a universe animated by love, restored in love, but he was not understood. His words implied enormous change, revolutionary shifts in values; they meant division, discomfort and the upturning of everything that was seen and safe.

When you and I were little, we were taught that we couldn't change the world. We were brought up to control ourselves, to conform, follow the norms, but our hearts

All Shall Be Well

were never made to rest in such conformity. Christ came like a whirlwind, like a storm and washed away the cobwebs; he called us into new life, a dynamic, creative co-authorship of a happier world. The time is now, the instrument of change is us, together, reaching out, lifting the broken and the injured into our arms, making them whole again. There is hope, we are that hope, there is witness and you are he. From the mysterious clouds and shadows that masked the words of the prophets and seers he came and breathed life into dying hearts. His tears made us live again and his blood flowed in our veins. From beyond he came into our world and broke the chains that bound us to fear and pain. He came to give his Spirit, his power to those who opened their hearts to him; his message was of new life, resurrection, the gift of joy, the gift of self, the gift of eternal happiness.

The difference between Christ and the Pharisees, the truth and falsehood, was that his words needed no credentials or proof. He came quietly and calmly, he demanded nothing, asked for nothing, judged no one. The Pharisees laid down the laws, enforced rigid beliefs, condemned the sinners – the righteous in judgement over the damned.

We, like Christ, are sent to love. Christ, the original missionary, walked and lived among his people. He did not need to wave a flag or prove his point, it was enough that he was serving his people, sharing himself; it was enough for them to see his example. A living missionary does not need to hand out pamphlets or label his flock, he simply serves, heals, listens and gives with joy. This was the way Christ lived and generated his truth, by deed, by action, by infinite kindness and patience.

We have the freedom to walk away like the rich young man. He will not change if we do not respond, his love is an invariable. His call to joy is unambiguous letting go of fear in order to live life fully. The promise, the covenant, was that if we let go of our petty distractions and

Christ, the Gentle Lover

mundane preoccupations, if we allow the Spirit of God into our lives, we will receive a new and radically different reality, a fulfilment and sense of presence – what theologians would call total spiritual and metaphysical conversion into grace.

The essence of Jesus' teaching was contained in the Beatitudes. He told persecuted people that they would be given joy. Those who tried to bring peace to each other would be God's sons; in realizing just how much love and help we need, we draw closer to paradise. The call of God is inevitably an invitation to help and serve each other, it is a call to laughter and humour, to seeing the goodness and healing the bad.

All over the world tonight there are persecuted and tortured people. There are oppressed and destitute people, victims of unjust systems that separate rich from poor. They are given the crumbs off the table. Half of humanity has known hunger and conditions beyond our imagination. The call of God is an invitation to stand by those who have nothing, to be the voice of the voiceless and the home of the homeless, to work constructively for a better world, with hands outstretched and mind wide open. The message of Christ is one of liberation and mercy, of compassion and non-violence. "Don't even become angry, neither shout at each other nor swear at anyone" . . . "Don't humiliate or punish another, because I love you too much." This Lord was intimate with our deepest feelings and emotions. He knows what is in our heart, what arouses us and excites us; he knows what terrifies and unnerves us; he is intimate with our private world, our fantasies and imaginings, our dreams and ambitions.

This Christ showed us how to love, showed us the true depth of humanness, never harming each other or taking vengeance, never beating or punishing, always cherishing and changing through tolerance and example. He never used his power over the weak, he only used it to make better, to restore. We too should only use our influence and power to build and bind, not to cripple or manipulate those around us.

We should never make another human being frightened or be the cause of tears (except tears of love). Our lives should slow down to make time for each other's needs, to listen, to be gentler. As God himself invites us: "Be still, and know that I am God" (Psalm 46:10).

His values are, of course, completely nonsensical in the fast moving business world of today. You don't get very far if you take him too seriously and all too often you'll get used and conned. It's true, the children of this generation are wiser and cooler and better off. But I doubt very much if they are happier. I look around me in our hut beside our clinic, in the middle of nowhere. Each night our growing family sings and dances, plays and finds room for ever more visitors who huddle near the open fire on the rough floor. It is hard to imagine a home so alive, and exciting and happy. All are terribly poor, some have to be specially cared for and have built little cow-dung huts beside us. I remember Christ's words as they sing and joke: "Blessed are you who are poor in spirit, for you shall see God." In the world at large, where the almighty dollar rules, it is a rather unusual idea to "give to those who beg from you, and help all those who come to you and ask something from you" (see Matthew 5:42).

Western society is in need of revolution – not political or economic revolution, but a revolution of the heart, a new understanding of what it truly means to give. There is so much we could learn from other cultures, much we need to change, and the cry comes from every sector and stratum of society for fresh hope, a new world, a better way.

All of us at some time or another have walked past the beggar in the street. I have stepped over hungry mothers begging for food with wasted children at their breasts. I

Christ, the Gentle Lover

have walked past and done nothing. We all take delight in sending our mother some flowers or a surprise, knowing the delight it will bring. We have at some time or another given a word of advice or support to a friend and know the good vibrations it gives us. There are many kinds of giving and notgiving, all sorts of reasons and motives. We usually give subjectively, and usually to those we know and love.

This is one of the big differences between us and God. He gives through inner understanding and from his abundance. He gives without restriction even to those who don't believe in him and ignore him. His unrestricted and boundless generosity showers us with gifts, many of which we fail to see.

Yet when we give, we often judge. "Is he worth it? He'll probably waste the money. Why bother", we justify ourselves. But as Kahlil Gibran so eloquently put it:

> Surely he who is worthy to receive
> his days and his nights is worthy to
> receive all else from you.
> And he who has deserved to drink
> from the ocean of life deserves to fill
> his cup from your little stream, and who
> are you that men should rend their bosom
> and unveil their pride, that you
> may see their worth. (*The Prophet*)

The deepest giving was the offer of Christ, the laying down of life for love, and he called us to give, in building a beautiful world. "Love those who want to hurt you and look down upon you, for you are the Sons of God. He makes the sun to rise on the evil and the good . . . Anyone can love those who love them. Love all my children" (Matthew 5:44–46).

The Word was made flesh and dwelt amongst us to give us purpose and life. The Word was not made flesh only on

All Shall Be Well

Sundays, but every day. The purpose of life was to be happy and full always, to taste life and partake of it in all its diversity and colour.

The paradox of being full is that to receive God we must empty ourselves, we must give, give time, energy, patience, service, touch, emotion, warmth, forgiveness, humour, silence. As Ecclesiastes says, there is a time for everything under the sun, even to give yourself, to receive, to accept, to let go, to cry and to laugh. The sacrament of giving is an openness to the whole gift of God, an experience of living through the Christ and the Spirit.

Our giving, whether it be a kiss, an act of love, a deed of kindness, a special favour, that costs us dearly, should be hidden and unseen. Like all goodness it speaks for itself, like all beauty it stands out on its own. Let your giving be a daily pleasure, a daily service in the least thing so that it will grow into everything.

Christ came with an earth-shaking challenge, a hope and a dream. He came, he forgave, he touched us intimately and gave us all those things that matter most. As well as this he invited us to do something else – to commune directly with God, to lift up our beings and relate to the eternal presence of creation. This act of love, we call prayer. It is a very exciting and ever-new discovery which, once embarked on, reveals only beauty and new hope and gives us endless courage and delight.

Prayer is not a dirgeful, monotonous activity, it is a passionate and dynamic movement of the depths of my being. It is the stirring of everything good in me and the caress of his hand as we grow in his light. Prayer is ultimately the only way forward to a better world since it is the door by which we become our better selves, it is the movement to the eternal in our little hearts, the dawn of the most sacred, dwelling in our fragile mortal beings.

Christ, the Gentle Lover

The language of prayer is the greatest of all paradoxes and enigmas. It has no words, there are no ideas or concepts that can even dimly reflect it; it is a touch, a sense, a part of us that is one step past the purely conscious. It is beyond will and imagination, it cannot be induced or measured or quantified. Prayer is the resurrection of God in you, the dawning of happiness. It is a cry in the dark, a burst of light, a glimmer of something unseen, a knowing of what is forever unknowable. The language of prayer is God himself moving in us, in our minds, our desires and actions and making them channels of his peace.

Whole libraries have been filled with countless volumes written about prayer. Mystics and saints, monks and sages, lamas and gurus have written about it; some have feigned it, others endlessly pursued it. It has been formulized, systemized, doctrinized, analysed, and we still don't understand it. For all the methods and techniques of prayer perhaps the simplest was spoken by Jesus himself: "Go in silence and in secret to your room, do not be seen – do not repeat words . . . lots of talk, your Father already knows what is inside your heart, He will answer you" (Matthew 6:6).

Perfect love needs no words. We speak often when we don't know what to say. His love runs so deep, his language needs to be listened to very silently to hear what he is saying above the noise and busyness that distract us. That is why over the centuries we have evolved styles of listening and opening our little lives to God. These practices we call meditation, reflection, contemplation, and, more generally, prayer itself.

The meaning of prayer in Christ, the essence of the actions of prayers, lies in the promise of Jesus to unite himself with us totally. His promise was of spiritual interfusion, of filling our lives and eternities with himself, by his Spirit. That promise was repeated endlessly through his witness on earth and has been reflected through his living actions and deeds of love ever since.

He did not say that it wouldn't be difficult and traumatic. He did not say that we would be free of pain, almost crushed, but he did promise that we would not be overcome and that he would always be with us.

The deepest form of love, the highest ideal, is as we have discussed, a concern for the "others" without looking for any return. It is an overflowing of happiness into the flux of life around us. There are many expressions of such love, and Christ reflected these in his short ministry.

We have so far touched on his simple teaching to serve and celebrate, we have mentioned the dynamics of his giving and the communion with God which we call prayer. Crucial to the Christ-gift to humanity is the cornerstone of intimacy and unity, a power to enter into the human struggle, to feel our weakness and know our deepest thought, to allow him to penetrate us more deeply than we can ever know ourselves.

When Christ loves, it is not only an outer cherishing, but a complete and whole *meta-noogenesis* going beyond spiritual growth and becoming, beyond the limits we have set, into the wordless experiences of interior knowing.

Empathy has two stages: firstly, Christ's empathy and depth within us, and, flowing from that, resurrection of self, our growing understanding and caring for the humanity we are part of.

Possessed of freedom and the intimacy born of the personal experience of a dynamic love relationship, the invitation of Jesus was to be his act of love and hope to mankind.

Implicit in his countless deeds of compassion and kindness was our reflection of such action explicity here and now. In the final analysis of Christianity today, it is not Christ who is seen as the example, but those who claim to follow his footsteps. We are, for better or worse, his living

Christ, the Gentle Lover

examples to the world. Our lives, by implication, claim to reflect something of the risen Lord. If I look into the busy hustle and bustle of my life and find it just as self-centred and preoccupied as those I criticize, just as benign and courteous, with no radical differences, then my example, my profession, may have become mere lip-service, may have lost the centre-point that diffuses light and love.

Jesus did not bring complacency. He did not offer a cosy way out. He did not ask for money and tell gullible bystanders that they were saved. Certain trends in some modern "commercial" denominations dilute Christ to a "saved by TV investment policy". That there are disturbing abuses of the Gospel is nothing new. There have always been "wolves in sheep's clothing" and it is ultimately our informed consciences that must discern which path to follow.

The life of Christ called his followers into the turbulence of the world, to serve, to reach out to others who were hurt and broken and weak. He called us to show that we follow his vision of the Kingdom of God, through our thoughts, words and deeds. So too would hypocrisy be seen and known by his followers' prejudices and deeds.

If we, like Mary Magdalene, accept the true spirit of the living Lord, we become a quiet, perhaps hidden, nevertheless visible light and hope. The depth of Christ living in us is seen in the quality of our mercy, acceptance, in the time we have for others. If Jesus managed to have time for the beggars and the lepers, surely we can find time for each other. How many times have you been in an office and been kept waiting needlessly because someone is acting the role of the busy executive, or gone home and had no time to play with your children? Time is often the most holy and precious gift we can give to each other, simply seeing the other as worthy of our space, our energy, our attention.

One of the more disappointing tendencies in the

All Shall Be Well

"successful" man of today is his lack of time, his inability to make space for his family or himself. Life is about making time, finding time, discovering time, time enough to be fully ourselves, fully present to each other and to the goodness and wholeness in each other.

The essence of Christianity is not believing that Christ is God, even the Devil knows that; it is taking the word of God and allowing it to become flesh in us. Like all birth, all change, it can be painful transition and revelation. For Christ to be at the centre, we have to tear down the walls that hold us back, dig up the buried emotions and yearnings, breathe life back into half-forgotten dreams, give of ourselves and keep giving.

Of all the gifts of Christ, the jewel in the thorny crown of love is that rare and most powerful treasure – real compassion.

As in the life of Christ, compassion is the gift of myself into your pain. I do not necessarily come with answers or knowledge, only with myself, and join you, share with you, try to bear your cross. It is strength bestowing understanding to another in weakness. It is standing by a man when he's down and everyone else is ready to kick him. It is, more explicitly, the entering of God into my life and using my being to heal, his Spirit making peace and clothing nakedness with understanding.

Of all the great virtues, compassion is the most sacred and the most desired by us all. Compassion is the highest and deepest form of humanity. It is the only weapon against hate and cruelty, bitterness and intolerance.

From his touching of the lepers and Gethsemane's sacrifice and agony, to his Passion and his resurrection in us, everything that was done by Christ and offered by him was from his strength and power.

There was a woman who had been unfaithful to her husband and, in the customs of the time, it was seen as a

Christ, the Gentle Lover

great sin and deemed to be a perverse act of adultery. She was dragged from her crime, and exposed in front of an angry mob of law-abiding citizens. She was terrified and alone, she was wrong and had been caught out. There was no mercy for her, she was to be humiliated and finally stoned to death.

All of us have at some time stood in the crowd and been ready to join in. At times we have known what it's like to be on the receiving end of a few stones ourselves. The people wanted to test Jesus and see if he defended the woman, or if he would condone their anger and uphold their judgement, which in themselves they knew were cruel. Jesus merely bent down and wrote in the sand. He listened to their agruments and their quoting of the law, their judgements and their sound reasonings, and they raged and grew more fierce and wild with every word; the woman stood alone, trembling in her emptiness.

Christ simply said, "Let he who is without sin cast the first stone", and he bent down and continued to write in the sand. What he is saying to us as to the angry crowd is: "Little ones, I have known you from your first breath, your inner secrets and darkest thoughts; there is nothing I do not see. Now you judge this woman, but you and I know your own weaknesses and coldness. No one else knows, but we do. Do you still want to look into my eyes and tell me you condemn someone else?"

Slowly, they went away one by one, ashamed by the knowledge of their own sins. At last, the woman stood alone before Jesus; as each one of us, she was human misery and fear standing before divine majesty and love. Our petty fury ceases before his peace and stillness. We, in our sin, in our doubt, in our rage, search, panic, implore, speak and cry out.

> But as I rav'd and grew more fierce and wilde
>   At every word,
> Me thoughts I heard one calling, *Childe:*
>   And I replied, *My Lord.*
>
> (George Herbert, *The Collar*)

As the woman stood that moment before Christ, she captured the infinity of time. The countless times every man and woman stands in need of such mercy, such reasonless forgiveness. Everyone in the world stands ready to judge, but Christ touched those people for a moment with truth.

She was a last left alone with Jesus — a man, a god, the almighty and infinite God who came not in thunder or in anger, but as the perfect and most tender and strongest of men. So she stood, as we stand, with our little anxieties and concerns, our demands and questions. But when the woman faced Christ, looked upon him, there were no questions, no concepts. She was experiencing absolute mercy and compassion. She stood before him and filled her emptiness and pain with the fullness of himself.

"Where are they who accuse you?"

"They have all gone, Lord." In the face of love, they went away leaving only the Lord.

"Neither do I condemn you. Go, sin no more," he told her.

In the story of compassion, where do we stand as it is lived in each life every day? Each of our lives is a Passion, a resurrection, a witness, a daily summary of the Gospel. Some days we are the Doubting Thomas, sometimes a Pharisee, often we are one of the onlookers. At times we throw the odd stone, or, like Judas, sell out. When we become most fully human and alive trying to give joy and love, we become more and more like the true man, the living Christ. For the Christian, life is in pursuit of that goal, the imitation of Christ, the coming to life in us of everything that is good through a life of consistent forgiving, giving and compassion; guided in prayer, nourished by his words of love, strengthened by each other, we can begin to give life of our very best.

As we look at the quality and direction of our own lives we see a lot of good, some rough edges, some bad moods and impulsive unkindnesses. We have all hurt and embarrassed people we love, all manipulated a little here and there.

In this life we also see a lot of commonplace things that tie us to the mundane and mediocre. The search for a God of intimate love can seem a little removed from going downstairs and staring at TV, and the expectations that press around us as soon as we put down the Gospel. A lot of it sounds great but a bit inapplicable to where we are just now.

Whatever else we feel and think or experience about Christ, the most important criterion for future living comes from our answers to two questions. The second question we will discuss later, as the first decides the meaning of the second.

Throughout his life, Christ was asked: "Who are you? Where do you come from? Are you a God? What are you? Why? Are you a king? Are you the Son of God? Are you the Christ?" All of us wonder – Pilate, Herod, the Samaritan woman, the disciples. Christ asked Peter: "Who is it that you say that I am?" Peter replied, amid the confusion and uncertainty of the others: "You are the Christ, the Son of God, the Lord of Heaven."

No matter how mundane or occupied your life is, or how preoccupied we all are in our own little journeys on earth as we move towards him, he asks us in the fabric of each day: "Who is it you say that I am?" If I truly believe you are the Lord, the Christ, the Son of God, I won't be angry or impatient, I will not race around, I will not hurt you in my brothers. If I truly believe that you are my living Christ and are here now, then my life will be full of passion and delight. I will not be torn by the anxieties of others or their opinions. If I know that you are the Lord of my life and that my eternity is inside you, I will not be afraid any more.

If he is the Christ, my doors will be forever open to him and I will welcome him without exception. Who are you, Lord? Where are you, Lord? It is dark and I cannot see. How do I know what to do? How can I trust you to make me happy? "I am the light of the world, little one." "I am the way, and the truth, and the life", "I am the resurrection" (John 8:12; 14:6; 11:25). "I love you more than you can ever imagine in your wildest joys, believe in you more than any man could believe in you. I am with you, even to the end of Time."

He is the same God who told Moses from the fire, "I am who I am" (Exodus 3:14). The same God who was "The *Alpha and Omega*, the first and the last, the beginning and the end." (Revelation 22:13).

But who is Jesus Christ? Now, here, where is he to be found? Certainly in the depths of our hearts, certainly in our silent celebration of all life in our intimacy as we look towards him. But in the vastness of the world he walks in many disguises. He is the child sitting in the subway waiting to sell himself to the highest bidder. He is the tiny wasted infant in my arms who has never known a full meal. He is the young boy who died in the open with no place to go, swollen and helpless, his father caring for him at his side. Christ walks among the camps of the hungry, and in the deserts among the thirsty. He is in the slums and sees the oppression of his children. He is in the prisons and feels the pain of a young man being tortured without mercy. The living Christ is in every tear, in every drop of blood. Just as he rises in each soul, so does he feel their crucifixion and suffering.

Who is Christ? This is not an abstract idea we can react to from the security around us; the question is not a collective anonymous enquiry. It is a challenge to my life. Where is

Christ, the Gentle Lover

Christ now, for me? How can I reach out to him and touch him and love him and grow closer to him? My hands may become dirtied by his blood, I might have to take from him his crown of thorns and wipe the sweat from his brow. I might feel his bruised body and cleanse his wounds. I might have to pull the nails from his twisted arms and stain my clothes kneeling in the dust.

To touch the Christ today is no different from then; it involves the same realities, the same reluctance. All over the world he lives in the lives of the poor and the crushed and the broken. In much of India, the street dwellers purposely maim their children by taking out their tongues, blinding an eye, to give them careers as beggars and earn the pity of passers-by. In the slums of Mexico City, children are victims of incredible and bizarre corruptions. Every corner of the world bears the wounds of Christ, and we are called to cast some light, some hope in such a world. We cannot touch Christ without first his touching us. We cannot be touched by him unless we let go of fear and allow him to move inside us.

In the context of these thoughts, the least we can say is that the only reason and meaning that can make sense of human pain and suffering in this world is Christ. No matter how deeply we go into theology, the mystery of violence and suffering, injustice and poverty, remains ever more confusing and beyond us.

The most we can say of Christ is that he can enable us to change the world — at least, our little corner of it. We can become someone very beautiful and kind for each other; sanctity, holiness, is attainable in ordinary life.

Jesus Christ experienced failures in human terms, slander, torture and humiliation. He was burnt, he trembled, he wept, he was at times all alone as in his terrible emptiness in Gethsemane. They ripped him, and committed deicide, and a great darkness fell over the earth and the Earth trembled and all was night (see Mark 15:33). When, if, God dies in our lives, the same darkness and nothingness surrounds us. When he is no longer part of our living, we begin to realize how barren life is.

He called us to do great things. His promise was an unspeakable and dynamic love. For the first time, he told us we were his beloved sons, and that our God loved us utterly. He promised that he would be inside us, in the deepest part of us. He promised intimate love, inner resurrection and a whole new vision. He promised that the Spirit, the sacred, would be within us, healing and making us alive with joy.

CHAPTER SIX

The Sacred Within

We have reflected upon the state of mankind. We have thought a little about some of the divisions and pains that afflict humanity today. Then, from our deepest hope, came our search for God, our desire to love and be loved. Within the human struggle we spoke of Christ and his vision and the intimacy he offered to us, a promise which he made real in his rising into new life.

Our thoughts inevitably turn to the relevance and impact of a Christ in my life. The sum total of theological and mystical writings find their value only in so far as they touch and inspire the human soul. So now we must look upon the offer that is given, the offer of love and how we might respond.

Christianity is meaningless unless it touches the whole of humanity, unless it challenges our actions and futures, our values and beliefs. The crisis of mankind today lies in the great divide between rich and poor, between what is said and what is done, what is preached and what is lived.

In my experience of people, there are two basic ways in which we approach the Godexperience: the "What can I get?" attitude and the "What can I give?" attitude. In a materialistic environment we are instinctively drawn towards a mentality that measures gains and profits. If we approach the God-relationship, or any intimate relationship, looking for what we will get, it will always be constrained by our own limitations and smallness. This chapter tries to look a little closer at the meaning of "Yes, I will walk with you", in a violent and disjointed society.

All Shall Be Well

We are reluctant to go too close to the edge of faith, to take too many risks. After all, what's the point in just getting hurt? The reason for laying our necks on the line is our response to Christ, our conviction that we are one family and that the only realistic reaction to life is to forgive, to pray, to serve. The meaning of life is to discover the hope, and in the hope find enough faith to get up when we fall and love once more.

No matter how overwhelming or terrifying a situation might be, it is only as frightening as our fears let it be. Suffering stops when there is hope; healing begins when we kneel down and wash the wounds of another; change begins when I get up and accept life with both hands, even if it means the wounding of those hands.

Our acceptance of Christ does not immunize us from human weakness and failure, it does not keep us from sinning, losing our tempers, but it does transform our lives into a dynamic act of becoming, a witness of a better world and a promise of things to come. Each day starts with a question, or rather lots of questions, but there's only one important one.

Do you love me?

If you believe that Jesus Christ has something left to say and do then what follows will make perfect sense. If your heart cannot accept that the Nazarene was God, then what we are about to say will seem rather meaningless.

When Jesus had returned after his death, he said to Peter, "Do you love me?" Peter, somewhat disturbed, replied, "Dearest friend, of course, you know I love you." So Jesus bade him then, "Feed my lambs." He asked Peter again, then again, and by the third time Peter grew distressed and said, "Lord, you know everything, you know that I love you" (John 21:17).

He asks us in every face we see, in every hour we live, in every place we move, "Do you love me?" If we say yes, then we should try as hard as we can to do what he would do. In the lives of the great saints there was a humorous patience; in times of anger or chaos they would stop, count ten, and look up. "What would you do now, Lord? Over to you?"

To love God is to love the most boring and irritating person you know. It is to forgive the most aggressive and hateful person you know. It is to let go of vengeance and jealousy, to be free of obsessions that fill your mind. At least, that's the theory. Most of the time, it remains the ideal. I remember once seeing a young girl, her face covered with blood, unrecognizable. She had been so badly beaten up by her father that she could not see. She was fourteen. It took hours to properly treat her, and during that time her father arrived. I didn't particularly feel like welcoming such a man in our home – in fact, I reluctantly held back one of our workers from some spontaneous mob justice. He laughed off the beating as the problem of a few drinks too many. I felt angry, and if he had touched the girl I probably would have dived on top of him. The point of the story is this, that the realities of life as experienced by us all are often far from the Promised Land. Our reactions too are far from the promised Lamb of God.

"Do you love me?" Yes, Lord, but I'd like to bash that maniac's face in. "No, little one, leave him to me. Bring peace, do not hurt him." But Lord . . .

"Do you love me?" Yes, but that's not really the point. Why did you allow that girl to get beaten up? Why didn't you strike him down or at least let him sleep it off? A lot of the time we talk to God this way, in human terms. Why Lord, for God's sake, why?

In Uganda a thirteen-yearold boy, Sebastian Nanduru,

was publicly executed, along with hundreds of thousands of others over the last decade. "Yes, I know. I was there, but do you love me?" I'm angry, Lord. It's all so cruel, all so hopelessly wrong. Why don't you do something about it, just look at . . .

Our answers become arguments, our silences become battlefields of freedom for people and social equality, they cease to be an opening and become a diatribe of what is wrong.

The Lord replies: "By the way, I did do something about all the pain and all the hurt." What? "I made you."

Every now and then we gain momentum and energy and do our best. There are times when we slide off, other times when, like the disciples, we tend to follow the tide. He says, "Will you also turn away from me?" and in our hearts we reply as they did, "But, Lord, to whom shall we go?" (John 6:66). We have nowhere else to go; he is our home, he is our origin and our destiny. Fortunately, though we often forget him during the day, he never forgets us, and while we might do something very bad, he never deserts us.

It is easy to say, "Yes, I really love you" to the Christ above the high altar. It is even easier to say, "Yes, I love you in those you send me to love", especially if I'm looking at a beautiful young friend. "But what about loving me in my other selves, do you love me then?" "Do you really love me?"

Tens of thousands live on the streets of New York and London with no place to go. Half of humanity goes hungry tonight in a world that has more than enough wealth. In a world of lonely people and pressured lives when can we find time to love ourselves, and everyone else, and him? "Where are you Lord?" We ask. "What do you want?" It all seems so confusing. Peter walked away from the chaos of Rome as an old man and was touched by the presence of his Lord. "*Quo vadis, Domine?* Where are you going, Lord?" he asked. Peter turned again towards Rome and to his death.

The Sacred Within

St Thérèse said that we could do nothing holier than his will, and we say so often, "Thy will be done." But his will is unpredictable, his desires at times charging wildly in the opposite direction to our own.

"Do you love me?" Yes, Lord. I am rich, I am healthy, I am OK. "Then feed my sheep." I'll write them a cheque, Lord.

"Do you love me?" Yes, Lord, I have enough to eat today. I have eyes to see. I have hope for tomorrow. I love you. "Little one, you are my lamb and I will feed you."

"Do you love me?" No, you have been rotten to me. I am sick, cold, poor, depressed. What have you given me? Nothing. No, I don't. You're not much of a God when you let so much misery happen."

"I understand what is in your heart, little one, and for now you do not see, but when you come into my Kingdom, you will know how I love you." Part of the riddle is that often in life we don't feel loved by God. We neither feel his presence nor his love. We just get bashed about from problem to problem.

Many years ago, the eyes of the world turned for a moment upon the Wolf Boy, found in the wilds and brought up by the wolves. In 1985, the Wolf Boy died at twenty-three years of age. His life among men had been a momentary curiosity, a great feature story, little more. He died in one of the homes for the destitute run by the Sisters of Charity.

He had been taken from what he knew and placed in an unfeeling world. So too do we often rob the innocent of their freedom and purity in the name of development. We make them anonymous so they look like us, we take away the magic. We change what is different to try and make it the same. We do not love, but manipulate. If a man dies never having loved it is a tragedy, because it means that he never experienced the gifts that God had placed all around him. If we really loved God, we would walk with him, we would stand at his side, we would never give in, and we would light a fire in our lives so as to wipe out unkindness. We would live the prayer of Dietrich Bonhoeffer: "Give me such love for God and men as will blot out all hatred and bitterness."

Where do we even attempt to love God? How? Whatever our perceptions, it is a daunting task, a heroic challenge. If the answer is a "no", then we are not yet ready to taste the mystery, or to dance the miracle, or to drink his blood and eat his flesh.

There is a tribe in Africa where Communion, the consuming of God, the "this is his body and blood", flows perfectly from their own belief of spiritual integration. It is an act of healing and restoration, it is the giving of grace. The African traditions (like the Prevedic schools of mystical thought and the later disciplines that evolved their own unique expressions of the sacred) have all contributed towards a more worthy notion of God. We cannot love God without first purging ourselves of a humanized God. We have to re-examine our understanding of how we see God.

One African tribe calls him "Nameless Whisper", another, "No Name", "Sacred Flame", another calls him "All That Is". In the great Eastern paths, the primordial concept of God persisted for centuries before being systematized over the last thousand years.

"Do you love me?" You are the fire that burns within me, you are the tears that fall upon my cheeks, you are the wind that enfolds me, you are the blood that pounds within me.

"But do you love me?" You are the silent touch, the awakened life within me, you are the dawn, the deepest part, the life, the death, you are what I am not, you are my sacred and closest breath. I do not see you, I cannot touch you, yet I feel you and I tremble in the darkness. I love you, I want you, I need you, you are my home, you are my

The Sacred Within

ecstasy, you are what is to be and what all men will become. You are love, and in as far as I, your frail child, can love you, yes, I love you. Help me in the weakness of my love.

We begin to move a little closer towards the nature of an intimate and passionate God once we strip away some of the traditional labels and concepts of him and draw closer towards the less familiar, less clear language that tries to evoke understanding. If we do attempt to try and love our Lord, we go to him not on our own but as part of the great power that is life. As the monk kneels in silent prayer, so too his heart lifts up the whole human race. As we find love, we find it through each other. As we answer a living breath, we discover the truth together.

Whatever may or may not happen after time, after the world is over, the most universal religious belief is that all things shall be drawn into the centre. Some say that the energy will find harmony in a nirvana or state of serene harmony, others that through cycles of purification and ascendancy we will attain an ultimate level of consciousness in an invisible higher reality. Still others talk of a Promised Land, a New Jerusalem where we shall all live in peace.

Whatever the words or expressions, at the core of most major religious beliefs lies an ultimate unity. This is often interwoven with some kind of judging of good and evil. Rather than venture into an examination of the apocalyptic traditions or theories of eschatology, let us concentrate on the predominant common point – unity.

In a Christian world, a really living Christian vision, there would be no loneliness, no violence, no rejection, no poverty. The dynamic of Christianity is far more radical than even the most idealistic Communism, which became a tragic suppression of free thought in a vain attempt to perpetuate a godless ideology. Any society that formally negates God must also negate the right of people to pray

All Shall Be Well

to such a non-existent delusion of the ignorant peasants. As is the case under all persecution, the pursuit of religion has thrived and grown in every corner of the world. Wars, hatred, adversity, always bring us together, which is probably why the Christian faith is so strong after centuries of oppression.

"Yes" to God means that we are prepared to serve, to go all the way. It implies a reversal of values, from I to you, from me and mine to us and ours, from the centre of myself to the centre of Christ in myself. "Yes" begins with welcome, begins with a drawing together. You are welcome, come within, draw closer. It is a basic warmth and trust of the rest of humanity. Hospitality, like so many of our customs, has been compromised by distrust, suspicion, territorialism. For God to dwell within us, we must welcome all his children to his home.

Sometimes we have much to learn from ancient traditions and peoples. The Maasai peoples, pastoral nomads of East Africa, live scattered over a vast area of Tanzania and Kenya. Their simple homes belong to all their peoples, anyone is welcome anywhere. It would be like us being able to sleep in any home in any city any time, and for it to be understood and taken as part of life, a joyful welcome. For the Maasai, every other Maasai is one of the family. There exists, as in much of Africa, a very loose interpretation of family, of brother and relations. Sadly, our definitions of home, family, brother, have become so restrictive that the primary family unit itself stands in jeopardy of further division.

Among the Maasai, mothers share children, legions of them. There is always that indissoluble bond between the child and the actual mother, but the other mothers, who all live together, give love and attention to all the children and share each other's work. If you admire the least thing in the home, it is given to you. I once admired a young child who was handicapped; hence we were given the child and through the village began to do a little for the retarded at bush level. Possessions have only one purpose – to be used by those who need them. When blankets, food and wood went from our clinics, I questioned one of my friends as to who he thought was giving the blankets out. "We all are," he replied, then explained the state of the people they gave them to. It was just the obvious thing to do, the only thing to do.

The future of us all ultimately depends upon our individual commitments to humanity, to family, friends, community, nation, globe. Togetherness is not built by closing the door at any one of these states, it slowly evolves during the gradual effort we make to love one another. This is not quite as easy as it seems. The struggle for equality, liberty and social justice often makes them become ends in themselves and we lose sight of the overall aim, togetherness. Human beings only change when they begin to forgive, when they learn the potency of selflessness.

One of the medieval images of hell and heaven reflected in simple terms the essential difference between hell and paradise. There was a great feast, and every kind of food and gift was there. The people were hungry and clambered over each other to get what they could. People were beaten and trodden underfoot, and in the end, amid the riots, they realized that all the food had suddenly gone, and that the food which they had already eaten tasted bitter.

The other place, heaven, was also the scene of a great banquet. There the great numbers sat together and fed each other, serving the smallest and the oldest first. As they ate, the sweeter the food became and there was great delight.

Of course, modern theology is reluctant to reflect sacred realities in such earthbound ways or to project human emotions on to God, but the point is clear. Heaven is a state entered into when we finally let go of our passing selves and celebrate as one body, one "mystical relation ship", in cherishing and understanding each other.

Hell is the attitude of putting me and what I want for myself before everything else. It is closing the door on joy, it is being buried with one's own potential and realizing what wasted opportunities for loving we had.

"Do you love me?" enfolds the more immediate and no less demanding question: "Do you love each other?" While looking upon the strife and violence of the world at large, we sometimes bow our heads in shame at how much men seem to hate each other and that more than half of the global budget is dedicated to weapons, armies and military spending.

When we look into ourselves, we see that we too pour a lot of energy and resources into self-protection and defence, in more subtle ways. The answer can only be a personal one, it can only be driven by my own commitment. The coming together of humanity begins with me and you, our overcoming of fear and scepticism, our walking through life in the spirit of St Francis, being channels of peace, instruments of kindness and generosity. Unity comes from the daily, hourly response to loving each other.

As with all intimate feelings, we are often confused and sometimes misguided in direction. So too with our response to God, especially our outward responses which initially are the mainstay of our religious expression. The simplest monitoring guide to knowing if we are on the right track lies in these questions: Does this fulfil me? Does it generate love? Am I open? Am I going outside my own boundaries? Am I learning?

It is important that we educate ourselves a little to know more about the Lord we are trying to follow. While we don't need to go deeply into theology or the theories of applied theosophy and exegesis of Scripture, we can learn a lot from the journeys of other frail people who have come from the same place where we live and have the same doubts and problems. This reflection can cover many expressions of experience, from the writings of Martin Luther King to the novels of Morris West, from the experimental Christology of Schillebeeckx to the simplest prayer we learnt as a child.

We understand God more as we open the window of wonder. The real response to the coming of something inside your heart is silent awe. Just as we don't read love letters to our beloved when we are together, neither do we read or analyse in the silences of our prayer. It is enough to be close.

There was a simple, almost illiterate man who failed most of his exams. He finally managed to get ordained a priest and was sent to a small town, where most of the people did not show any interest in the Church. The broken-down parish chapel was empty, the valuables long since removed, as had been the lead on the roof. It was here that John Mary Vianney spent most of his days and nights. He would visit the people, would help wash and feed the children of mothers who were busy at work. He would preach to the empty church every Sunday – empty, that is, apart from two old sisters who came faithfully each morning for Mass.

John would sit for hours at the back of the church, silent and content. When asked why and what he did there he replied, "I look at him, he looks at me." He said there was no secret to prayer, that simply being there was enough. The strange simplicity of this man and his understanding of God brought back the sceptics and the lost, the young and the middle-aged. His chapel became one of the most visited places in Europe, and the *curé of Ars* the most loved parish priest in the world.

Such saints manage to go all the way, the rest of us meander around a little. As A. de Bovis put it: "The mass of humanity keeps moving forward. There is a small, closely knit nucleus. The rest follow behind in a haphazard way, doing the best they can . . . But they do follow."

All Shall Be Well

Most of us are like St John Vianney. We strive to look at him and that's our effort at prayer, simply being there. If we allow this to deepen and grow, it will create in us a serenity and inexplicable harmony born of a humble emptying of ourselves to his kindness. This act of love, this sowing of his seed in us, has many names, and has no explanation. For want of another word, it is the kiss of Christ, the bestowing of grace, the act of Pentecost.

Understanding and interpreting life translates into seeing love moving in its own strange way through our lives.

There is pain in the world because of greed, because of the lust for power and the myth of self-importance and pride. With all our inhibitions and taboos we still frown upon sexual deviances and practices as the great sins, yet vanity and ego are infinitely more destructive.

We cannot see God's will in our lives unless we become like the children who run naked and free. Our response to God comes gradually in how we treat each other. We only begin to see where and to what God is calling us when we have the courage to let go of everything into prayer, into that oddest of all human endeavours, talking to someone we cannot see or feel.

The miracle occurs when you begin to realize how important you are to God, to his plan, to the future of mankind and the coming of paradise. You are, in effect, the only one made, the first and last; "you", your self, is one of a kind, rare and irreplaceable. You are, to summarize Christ's message, the most precious and wonderful of his creations. The moment that your thoughts, your distractions and wanderings are lifted up, the moment the whole of you becomes present in a single second of time, the moment you sincerely abandon one thought or word unto the hidden, is the moment it touches the ears of God. It is this intimacy, this moment, which is your deepest prayer, for at the moment your words come from your heart, your thoughts free of yourself, you are in the grips of prayer.

It would not be so hard if Christ stood before us, the naked body of our prayer, breathing his breath and knowing his secret, his side open and bleeding, our fingers touching the open hands. We could understand if he came among us. All around us the hidden moves and signs, yet the whole earth heaves to the sound of banging as new crosses are forever hammered together and Christ is lifted time and time again to his death.

Our response to God in the world is to reach out into him, to embrace him, to identify him, yet at the same time not become swallowed up into the chaotic rush of life wherein he lives, breathes and has his being with us.

We begin our response to life in prayer, the prayer that is the torn tissue of daily life. We deepen and mature our own horizons through silence and patience, through reflection and seeing the hidden in the habitual occurrences and routine of ordinary life.

Understanding comes from an attitude, a way of looking at things; it comes from seeing and doing things a certain way. The core of the secret is patience and trust. In the words of Teresa of Avila:

> Let nothing disturb you,
> Let nothing frighten you.
> Everything passes,
> God alone is changeless . . .
> Who has God, wants nothing else,
> because alone, he is everything.

We understand through the often painful failure of experience, through the let-downs and betrayals. Yet we understand God in and through his workings in humanity, his heaving in our hearts, in his act of love, lost within our most secret silence.

There are few words that evoke such potency and meaning and intimacy as does the word "touch". Touching, caressing, embracing, enfolding, indicate private and terribly personal aspects of friendship and love.

The word "touch" also denotes something else. In the context of me searching for God, it reflects a personal and direct experience of someone or something beyond me. The action of God in response to our prayer, and our response in turn, is what the dynamics of inward stillness are all about.

Prayer can at times be the loneliest, most frustrating and exasperating of experiences. It can be dry and boring, disillusioning and monotonous. The hours of attempted prayer can become very dark, and this is an experience common to us all. As St John of the Cross' "Dark Night of the Soul" tells of Christ's desolation in Gethsemane, we all know something of the nothingness and loneliness of prayer. Sometimes this attempt is the deepest and most sincere prayer of all. "For God's sake help me. I don't know what to say or where to turn. Help!"

For some, God comes like a bolt of lightning, or a torrent of ecstasy. Most of us, however, experience little flickers of light, little moments of warmth. Sometimes God seems dull and ordinary in his expression, yet his touch is always enough to give us strength to go on.

Unless a man experiences in his own life something of the holy, it will always seem to him that the sacred is only a façade, a lie. There are many people critical and cynical of the pursuit of the sacred, sceptical of the spiritual. To some people it is both naïve and unrealistic to follow the Gospel of Christ in such a way as to transform the acceptable norms of life. The touch of God is often viewed by a sophisticated society as impractical idealism. The movement of God is dismissed by such people who become so caught up in their own busy routines and acts that they carefully avoid any solitude for fear of their own self-doubt.

Jesus Christ reaches so far into our crippled insides that he gives reason to the madness, purpose to monotony, hope where before there was only uncertainty. Christ came into a world of smart men, cynics, experts. He came into a system which was dominated by proud people. The world has changed little since then. The struggle between pride and kindness, arrogance and peace, continues, the unending war between good and evil, joy and sorrow, healing and pain.

We are caught in a world where God kisses us and touches us, yet where men are crippled by the obscenities of poverty and violence. Does God touch the rich man in his cosy home with the same hand as he touches the abandoned old woman? Christ came amid the poverty and pain, but he did not change it, he left that for us to do. There is little good in divine enlightenment or being born into the Spirit, little meaning in the familiar words of the saved, unless those words are made flesh by our deeds.

Those who experience the purging, unsettling touch of God inevitably reflect a quietude and determination to do something, rather than merely lift up their hands in prayer. When a man is beaten down, homeless and sick, when he is on his knees, do we tell him to join his hands in prayer or do we lift him up?

The action of God in our lives calls us into action in the lives of others; his touching of our hearts impels us to touch the plight of those around us. We cannot have intimacy at the price of privacy. Our intimacy with a living, powerful, throbbing creation draws us into a deep "knowing" of what is the wholly other, and a strong commitment to the whole of humanity which is woven and linked into our love affair with God.

All Shall Be Well

We are estranged by the noise around us, constantly distracted by the machine world of which we are a part. The simplest experiment to illustrate the point is for you to close your eye and stay still for a single hour. In the minutes that follow you will experience a tidal wave of worries, thoughts, things to do. In that hour you will experience and taste relatively little of your real self. Like swimming, learning a language or any art, it takes time and practice.

A great saint, famed for his powers, was once asked: "Why do you pray so much and study so much on prayer when you have already reached such heights?" The saint smiled and replied: "I think I might be slowly making progress." A world-famous violinist was being congratulated upon his masterful concert performance. A zealous lady lauded him: "I'd give my life to play like that." He replied: "My dear madam, I did."

Silence is a language, the language of listening. It requires a great deal of time, trust and patience. Truth requires the investment of our whole lives. If God speaks in my life, if the unseen acts in me, I must be calm and collected enough to taste his action, to intuit the subtle motions of an invisible and unfathomable love.

When God touches our flustered hearts, his understanding is such that there are no words, just a deep happiness and warmth, a very strong surety. There are times when I have been frustrated and angry with God, furious at the pitiful misery of children around me, the squalor, the disease, the hunger. We vent our rage at God and his indifference, but then the anger dies to his embrace, his deep waters that silently flood our frantic minds. His touch is just that, it is not a defence, a reasoning, an explanation, it is not an answer or a solution, it provides no retort to our demands. His touch is nothing other than an inner restoration of balance, a moving of the Spirit inside us, the brooding of God in the abyss.

The Sacred Within

We are, of course, all touched by God all the time. He is very deeply a part of us in all we do. The holy night, the moment of Christ's birth, is when he appears, when he stirs in the feverish activity of life. There is an old Christmas carol that reflects the most radical liberation theology in its stark simplicity.

"Long lay the World in sin and air a'pining full of tears. Till he appeared and men felt their worth, the thrill of hope. The weary world rejoices, for now begins a new and glorious dawn . . . hear the voices. In all our trials, born to free our hearts."

The realization that he has come with all of heaven to find us, that the universe awaits our response, that his arms are about to lift us up, is the central core of all theology. No matter how bloody human history, no matter how stained our own conscience, no matter how dull or guilty our past, the breaking of the dawn has come, the resurrection of the soul is now, in the littleness of our hearts as they accept the power and gentleness of the incarnate God. This acceptance, this stirring of life within us, depends upon a readiness to shift our life base, our axis.

Traditional ways of expressing love's entrance into our lives were rather gloomy and emphasized words such as repentance, remorse, confession, penitence. What this language refers to is simply knowing ourselves as we really are, our self-righteousness, our moods, our tempers, our weaknesses. In that knowledge we are to look far within us and see what we are called to be and believe in the potency of love inside us.

There was a man who had worked for many years with the downtrodden. He went away for a few months to rest and build up strength. He had become tired by years of rough living. In the time he had alone, he was asked to feel sorry for all his sins. He wanted to ask, "What sins? I am sorry for the little mistakes I have made but they are part of me." Some time later he was saying Mass, and heard the words: "Be not afraid, I go before you always, give me your hurts and burdens. I will lift you and comfort you now." It was at this moment that he realized that sorrow for one's sins is more sorrow for how little we live his joy, how little we accept his offer of friendship in the spirit of total trust.

Christ spoke of the humble tax collector who stood at the back of the temple and beat his breast saying, "God be merciful to me, a sinner." We have all met such people, who look upon God's face with faith and unshakeable trust, those who can say, "Lord, I believe, help thou my unbelief."

We do not know why there is pain, why there is such hatred and violence. We are not certain about anything and walk in the footsteps of one whom we believe knew the way. No matter how far we reason things out, our response to God does not come from the head but from the stuff of which life is made, blood, guts, sweat and tears. It comes from the heart without provocation or reason. Like all communion, the trust, the holding of hands, involves both of us, him and me.

The scene was a dark and stinking barracks. The rabbis had gathered, shaven heads and in prison rags. About them their chosen race was being twisted and destroyed in the camp. The rabbis debated whether or not God had deserted them, whether he had left his people to this bizarre fate. After great discussion they agreed that perhaps God had deserted them and had gone away or had died. They fell silent and about them the feverish hum from the camp scarred the silence. Then the oldest among them said: "We have decided that God is dead and has deserted us. We too are to die. All is lost, now, let us pray . . ."

The presence of God lives in the sacrament of the present, whatever the present may be. We are, of course, to stand up and be counted, to break down what is evil and corrupt through mercy and kindness. The only lasting furrow through history has been the resilience of love in

The Sacred Within

the midst of endless wars, the deeds of compassion in a world of greed. One single act of human goodness conquers all else.

Do we remember the name of the Emperor of Rome, or the kings of the earth 2,000 years ago, or the great generals or reformers, or even what empires existed? No, we only remember a tiny infant born in a hovel, who lived in simplicity and spent much of his life in obscurity. Christianity, like all sacred truth, lies in the reality of God's action in men; not in saints or sages, but in each of us indiscriminately, regardless of who or what we are.

In his strange, almost mystical short stories, the much-persecuted Oscar Wilde recounted the invisible workings of God. One story tells of the selfish giant. He built a great wall round his garden to keep out the children. But then his beautiful garden fell under the power of winter and the birds no longer sang in the trees. The story tells of how he encountered a tiny child in a far corner of the garden where the infant was playing up a tree. The giant, moved by the joy of the child, broke down the walls of the garden. He fell in love with the wondrous boy and, over the years that followed, hoped that the little boy would one day return to see him. The garden was always full of happiness and the laughter of many people.

The giant grew very, very old. Early one morning he went walking as dawn slowly stirred the garden into life. Then, in the far corner of the garden where years ago he had seen the wondrous child, there amid the blossoms of the tree stood the infant, unchanged, radiant as ever. The giant was overjoyed. As he gazed upon the child his eyes filled with tears, then his face grew red with anger and with all his might he cried out. For there upon the little hands of the child gaped deep wounds that ran with blood. He drew his great sword and cried, "Who hath harmed thee thus, for I shall slay him." The giant trembled with rage.

The little boy smiled and lifted his arms. "My friend,

these are the wounds of love. For many years you have let me play in your garden. Come now and play in mine." The giant knelt and took the child in his arms. They found his body under the great tree covered in blossoms, for he had gone to play in his Father's garden.

There are many possible responses to life. We are deluged under mountains of questions all the time. Some are predictable – career decisions, friendship opportunities. Others land on us like a storm – death in the family, accidents, illness. How we react to the multitudes of crises, problems, rows, dilemmas and choices depends on our interior answer to the Spirit of God who offers to celebrate life with us. How we answer life and those around us depends upon the deeper answer of our hearts to the gentleness of God and how we accept his moving in us.

Many people postpone an answer, hoping for more proof, or a better deal with God. We compromise the most important relationship of all, our communion with God, for fear it will upturn our lives, and indeed it surely will. "I want to love you, Lord," we say, "but I cannot. I need you, but not yet. I will serve you, but cannot walk all the way yet. Later, after you have given me the strength. I am afraid, Lord, I do not know, I can not see you. Why don't you give me some sign, some help . . . ?"

Our "yes" is not so much a plunging into the far reaches of contemplative prayer as a reaching out of a trembling hand to another person. As we have said, it is how we live and behave with each other. Expediency and convenience for the sake of our comfort cannot compromise the true meaning of Christ's words, nor their implications and effects in our lives.

St Francis kissed the leper, Vincent de Paul lifted up the destitutes and gave the outcasts his own bed. Christ welcomed them all. In an enlightened society, we have

The Sacred Within

reacted to our shame less worthily. Those slowly dying of AIDS and associated diseases have been not only ostracized but have experienced a phenomenon of such isolation as has not been experienced since the treatment of lepers in Europe in the thirteenth century.

We alienate what we do not understand. Our own protectionist policies in many spheres of life reflect values radically apart from the precepts of compassion inherent in Christ. We who would be called the followers of Christ are, in reality, the city set on the mountain, the salt of the earth, the light, the hope. We are his instruments and his hands. Of course we are unsure at times, but we must err on the side of giving rather than on the side of reason.

When I first saw a dying man, he was filthy and wasted. His moanings were helpless muted cries and I felt like running away. The impulse to flee was so real that I took a few steps back. The man was about twenty-five and looked closer to fifty-five. I was thinking more of my own fear than his as I sat beside him. I could not speak to him. I felt helpless and pathetic. Yet he seemed happier that I was there. By the morning he had died, and as he passed from my presence he doubtless felt the touch of blessed hands lifting him into life. The only answer in the face of death is compassion, and a faith born of one's own experience of the hidden. Without this experience we are terribly afraid and naked confronting the last and final void.

Death is the realm of the sacred, not the realm of medicine. It is when humanity embraces its deepest meaning and destiny. It is our transformation into the unseen and divine when we become our complete selves.

"Yes" means that I will go all the way. I will risk my life in one unabated "yes" to the whole human miracle. If I reply "no", I will live in the small bubble of myself, neurotic, forever looking for someone, something to fill me.

If I say "yes" on my terms, I will pray on Sundays, satisfy my wants and needs, put myself first and cling to what I see. Our only hope is the "Amen" of life, the laying of my humanness and existence in the unseen hands of God, knowing that he will mould me and create in me only what is beautiful and strong, he will breathe into me light and courage, fire and passion, a passion that can embrace the whole diversity of creation without judgement or limitation.

Life is nothing without growth. We grow only when our hearts are answering the call to love, when we are responding to his call to love him and each other, to be united as one family in one act. This we learn through patient understanding and prayer. Our good will translates into actions not theories only when Jesus Christ begins to live in our actions and deeds.

Our reaction to the pulsating world depends upon how the Word becomes flesh in us. Our reaction to each other lies in the depth of love that has grown from honest and naked prayer. The Scriptures and great writings are just words unless they are lived between you and me. The Kingdom of God starts here and dies the moment it ceases to be the core of our lives, only to be born once more when we try to love again.

If you get up tomorrow morning and count all the people you meet in the course of the day, the children, the elderly, the boring and the pretentious, the friends and family, the big shots and the tramps, the shopkeepers and passers-by . . . In a single day we encounter a microcosm of humanity. We are made not only to love them all, but to cherish and comfort them all, even that 3 per cent who are a total pain in the neck. As John's first letter tells us:

> Beloved ones, Let us all love one another because we are all his children. If we do not love, we cannot know God, because . . . He is Love. Beloved, surely if God loves us, we should love each other.
>
> (1 John 4:7)

The Sacred Within

If the mystery of life is to dwell inside us it means simply that we do everything we can to love. If the sacred is to be experienced then it is through God's gift of love and joy celebrating the miracle of life in us. For the sacred to become alive, to become flesh and blood, we are called into a demanding and beautiful act of love, a love which is a great "yes" to life and a dynamic response to humanity and its Author.

CHAPTER SEVEN

The Dynamic Response

Living with God, deepening into union with him, does not happen overnight. Good intentions help, the external props can be of comfort, but the vibrancy of our living the Spirit into our own lives comes in the simple "Yes, I will walk with you . . ."

We are thinking creatures, sexual creatures, sometimes temperamental and often vulnerable. We are highly prone to injury, emotional and physical. We are invited to be living spirits, creative acts of Christ to a world which stands pining for hope and encouragement. You are that hope, that power, and God himself speaks and acts through you.

The response is simple enough. It can be summarized in the Desiderata, the thoughts of Tagore and Gibran, in the Beatitudes or in Augustine's "Love, and do what you like."

A healing life, a deeply holy life, is enflamed by three fires. The first is silent listening and communion with the presence of God, what we call prayer and contemplation. The second is the power of giving, serving and caring, which is really God giving through our hands. This is the fruit of love. The third flame is the mystical flame of God alive inside us, speaking, healing, touching and celebrating through us in the garden of life.

If our reflections begin to make us change, the process often begins in the brain as we think: "There might be something useful here." We criticize and examine the arguments and evidence, we measure it by our own experience of life, and if it appears to make any sense, we allow it to colour our impressions and opinions. Such is the human rational process by which we try to move towards "knowledge" and "insight".

Because of the need for some structured pattern to the way we think, various schools of thought and methodologies have evolved to help people understand and examine more clearly the place and meaning of God acting in their lives. One such school, Ignatian spirituality, developed a practical method of self-examination and discernment to help people to become better human beings. One useful part of the "Exercises" was a period in the morning and evening of silent evaluation of the day's activities. In the morning, I consider all the things I'd really like to do, in the evening, all the things I did. Of course, our intended responses often differ greatly from our behaviour. Such mental exernises help us to know ourselves a bit better and to see the direction of progress we are making.

If we are in love, we do all we can to know more and more about the one we are in love with. While books help, they are nothing compared with experiencing God directly. If you make the decision to love Jesus of Nazareth, you owe yourself the time to be present to him.

If you and I are to be found guilty of being Christian, then our actions and behaviour must mark us. If we are to go so far then we owe it to ourselves to understand more about what we are letting ourselves in for. In our meagre efforts to understand, we evolved theologies, philosophies, Christologies and lots of other specialized areas. The problem with these sciences is that they have become so specialized and technical that they are often light years from where most people think and live.

Theology is merely the reflection of man's relation-

All Shall Be Well

Theology is merely the reflection of man's relationship and union with God. All of us who question are theologians in the fullest sense and we should all be awake and ready to deepen and share our understandings. Would that we were like the one leper from the ten who came back and thanked Christ. Not knowing who he was, he returned without anything, full of thanks. "You are great, you have made me whole. Thank you." That's a reasonably accurate summary of theology, or at least what it's meant to be.

Of course reason only takes us a little bit of the way. The real change, the real movement, is an act of love and all love has that annoying tendency of denying the rational and reasoning processes. The best that we can get from thinking about Christianity is this: that in the light of the facts and evidence around us in the experience of life, Christianity is both a reasonable and valid response to the mystery of death, pain, love and hate, and the paradoxes that enfold daily existence.

The "Yes" of the mind is the springboard from which we dive into faith. Such faith has no reason, it is hard, it is hoped, it is unknown.

Our everlasting self, that part of us which is unseen, is, like God, a spirit. It can remain buckled up and buried or it can grow to embrace all creation. As God's child, I am irrevocably part of God's children. As long as some of us are crushed under the weight of poverty and violence, all of us will be in pain. The soul is not that part of life that is removed from the real world, it is the exact opposite. Our souls are capable of knowing the sorrow and pain of humanity above and beyond reason.

If our lives are to become full of happiness and remove despair and anxiety in others, we must become a generating station of hope and kindness. This peace comes from within, it cannot be learnt. It does not come with thunder,

The Dynamic Response

it comes from long hours of patient waiting, discovering a different realm of reality, a separate reality free of fear. The problem in talking about the "Yes" of the soul is that it is beyond the language of words.

One day we were burying a child who had died from malnutrition. We had done whatever we could do, to no avail. The tiny child lay in the hole, on her side as if she was asleep. The sun was scorching, and as I stood there and took in the futility of the situation I wondered what language could ever express what people really feel. The simplest prayer that followed translated into: "She comes from you, you take her back. What is yours is only yours, not for us to know, only to love. We thank you." After the anger that one feels in a world where a child can die like that, after the frustrations and the passing moods, there remains the simple truth, so hard to swallow, that we are all in the palm of God's hand and we are his. Life is his to take and give.

Just as God invites us to be one inside his spirit so too does he invite us to take up the cross, to lift up our pain, to drop it at his feet and let him bear it. The language of the soul, the language of love, is the reaching out of both hands in stillness. It is beginning to see the vast abundance of goodness all around us, to see with the eyes of the inner self. This reaching out is "contemplation".

If we took a few minutes each day to drain away the bile and the frailty, to let go of the pettiness and see only what is beautiful, we would experience the most traumatic and profound changes in the most mundane and ordinary things around us.

There is an old man incontinent and pathetic, dirty and senile. He lies on a pallet in a hospice. One man looks upon him as a liability and a problem for his family; they can't keep him or care for him. Another man looks and sees a patient, needed for analysis, diagnosis. Another sees an outcast, one of thousands ready to beg from him. Another sees a potential feature story. Another sees the face of God.

The "yes" is "Lord be in my mind and in my imaginings, be in my eyes and in my seeing, be in my body and in my loving, be in my touch and in my embraces. Be in my thinking and in my reasoning, be in me in the least thing I do, when I walk, when I sit. When I forget you, stay very close. When I hurt you or discard you, be inside me, never leave me. Show me how to see with your eyes and do with your hands and heal through your touch. Lord, when I am angry be calm in me. When everything crumbles to pieces and I hate everything, make me whole, let me see you in everything. When I panic, call me."

Like any love affair, you begin to feel and know how beautiful you are and how much you really matter when the one loving you gives you a sense of belonging. You are beautiful because you are the hand of God, the only one child he has. In you he has given a special miracle of uniqueness. Nothing can take away the fact that there is only one you. Beauty is not some Adonis or a breathtaking girl, not soft skin or deepblue eyes. It is the power that is inside you ready to shine. "Beauty is life when life unveils her holy face, but you are life and you are the veil. Beauty is eternity gazing at itself in the mirror, but you are eternity and you are the mirror" (Kahlil Gibran, *The Prophet*).

The acceptance of love is the burial of all those pathetic, lingering wounds from our past; it is when we become free from the guilt that limits our enjoyment and experience of life. A lot of deeply disturbed people, including young people who have dropped out of society, have allowed their circumstances and situations to affect their whole being. They have integrated and woven the pain of rejection or hurt into their own self-vision, they have not

The Dynamic Response

found a different vision, or tasted the beauty of being made new in a healthy life. Jeremiah talks of the soul's acceptance of the joy of life. "I found your words ... I ate them and tasted that they were so full of beauty and joy. And I was lifted up because I bore your name, you gentle one ... You bring what is precious from the worthless, and when I return to you, you make me whole again, and restore me" (Jeremiah 15:16, 19).

We find God, not divorced from the world, but intimately part of it. We find him in a face, in a moment of music, in the long haul of daily chores, in the street, in the most unexpected and common of places. We find him in the heights of the heavens and in the depths of our doubting hearts, in the world's confusion and noise, and in the bright darkness of inner prayer.

Mental prayer, meditation, stillness, tranquil abandonment, silent intimacy, Zen, Raga Yoga, solitude – different facets of the same diamond. The most important jump in life is the way we jump into prayer, or rather wade through it. It can be the most frustrating and stupid of all activities, and there are times we think it's a total waste of energy.

In America and Europe churches are empty, churchgoing has dropped consistently, an and air of scepticism has accompanied secularism. A lot of this reaction is not so much a rejection of institutionalism but an ignorance of where to start, how to begin, how to make it real. We don't know what to say. We don't want to use books, or someone else's words. But because we don't know what to say or how we ought to pray, "the Spirit himself intercedes for us with sighs too deep for words" (Romans 8:26).

But how do I know that I'll "trust that he is inside you and that he will take you by the hand"? (Proverbs 3:6).

All Shall Be Well

The only reply needed is the inner yielding and accepting. Let him hold you, let him take the lead. As Ignatius Loyola put it: "Pray as though all depends on him, and act as if all depends on you." Stripping ourselves naked in front of nothingness, listening to the silence, can be very frightening; this is what the saints called the dark night of the soul. It is the time when we feel very small and insignificant. We all know how boring and tedious prayer can be. The best we can say sometimes about our efforts is "I am here." It's a bit like arriving at an international airport with your bags when there's no one to collect you. You feel really lost and dejected just standing there hoping someone will charge over to you and give you a big welcome. Prayer can be a bit like that – an interminable wait, waiting for someone to call our name. Often such prayer ends in panic or dissipates into daydreams and fantasies.

Despite the unwanted thoughts and emotions, "He comes, calming the storm, and makes the wars end ... I am here, be still, and know that I am God" (Psalm 46:10).

But, Lord, look over there. Don't you see him, he's ...

"Listen to me in silence little one" (Isaiah 41:1).

But I don't feel very comfortable, Lord. I feel really uneasy. Listen ...

"Don't be afraid, come to me, I will love you" (Matthew 11:28, 14:27).

I am so weak, Lord. Help me. I am too occupied with trivial things and so many silly thoughts. You must think I'm so shallow and useless sometimes, and ...

"Deep calleth unto deep" (Psalm 42:7).

What can I say?

"Ask and it will be given you" (Matthew 7:7).

Everything is a gift, everything is promise. The words are personal love letters to you, secrets that find a private meaning in you. In the silence there comes a warmth, a

The Dynamic Response

chemistry, a quietness that is incommunicable and yours alone.

Like real friendship, the deeper the bond grows, the less need for words; the more open and familiar we become, the more pleasurable and delightful the experience. The more trust we lay down, the deeper we are touched. There is everything to gain, all we need is to open our lives to taste the touch. If you remember the times when you have been really over the moon with happiness, you want to share it; so too with the experience of inner joy. As it is wordless, the only way to share it is to try and love those about you.

He will love us whatever our response, and nothing we do will waver the consistency of his kindness.

No matter how down we get sometimes, with the tiniest grain of faith we are rescued. He demands nothing, there are no ulterior motives or strings attached, just love and an invitation to be happy. St Bernard felt the love of Christ all about him and wrote a lot about the love song of Solomon, which contains this profound truth: "You are beautiful. Turn away your eyes from me for they disturb me" (Song of Solomon 6:5).

Despite our betrayal and fickleness, our endless failures and hidden thoughts, he takes our trembling hand and says "Let us out early to the vineyards . . . There I will give you my love" (7:12). The last line of this, the most mystical of the books of the Old Testament, is: "Come now, it is you I love, my Beloved, I will love you." This is the offer to your life, to my life, that in our shared gift we allow ourselves to be the home of God, the garden of love, the instrument of peace.

Born from the depths of prayer, the conviction of reason and the simple step-by-step response to the beauty of God, we are called into action. The most important and essential criterion of being a Christian is what we do and what is at

All Shall Be Well

the centre of what we do. I have purposely avoided the word "charity" up until this point because the word has come to mean something very different in today's world.

Charity now has almost the connotation of big business, a profession – "the charity industry". It can also imply, to some people, negative motives for giving, trying to score points in heaven. It has become one of those distorted words, bereft of most of its essential meaning. Nevertheless, selfless giving without looking for anything back is the dynamism and fire of Christlike behaviour. The "action" and "yes" of life isn't a crusade or a campaign to convert people, it consists simply in giving, supporting, affirming, seeing what is good. The people that touch us most are those who heal, build, and give us a sense of our own worth. The essence of Christ is to reawake and discover our personal mystery. Like Simon of Cyrene, we must help each other to carry the cross, to love people where they are, not seeking to change or modify them, simply love them.

One of the most destructive attitudes we can have in relating to each other, is attempting to change or alter them to our own views. We are simply to serve and that can be very hard. The "yes" of Christ is "yes" to you. It is "I am with you, I trust you, I believe in you, I am here and living your mystery with you". It is the internal Amen. Our "yes" is simply to see good in everything.

There was a man called Damien, a simple priest who lived about a century ago. He lived and worked in a leper colony among people who were not wanted. Long before the changes of the Vatican Council, Damien had adopted a very personal way of saying his Mass. One morning he began the Gospel:

". . . So that all may be one, as you are in me I am in you . . . So they all may be in us and we in them as one – You sent me and loved them as you love me and we are in them . . ." (John 17:21, 23). Damien's long contact with the lepers had finally made him one, and his sermon began

The Dynamic Response

with the words: "My brother and sister lepers, we are one and he is in us . . ."

The "yes" of faith is the embracing of the collective reality that is life. "For I was hungry and you gave me food, I was thirsty and you gave me drink, I was a stranger and you welcomed me, I was naked and you clothed me, I was sick and you visited me, I was in prison and you came to me" (Matthew 25:35, 36).

The meaning of Christian life goes on into the smallest and most insignificant acts of patience, mercy and love.

When I was embarrassed and felt stupid, you encouraged me. When I had unbearable sorrow, there you were beside me. When I did that very bad thing and everyone condemned me, you offered me refuge. When I was cruel and cursed you, you forgave me.

To live a fully Christian life in today's world is hard, painful, demanding and often confusing. One feels like screaming, or just giving it up as impossible. But it is fulfilling, it lifts men out of the bloodshed and the mindless violence of a distraught age, and calls them sacred, children of God, children of hope and light. It ordains life into miracle and through our actions others will see the coming of a Kingdom. We are hope, we are life, we are love, we are the daughters and sons of love and everything that the future holds is the miracle of the coming of that love.

The greater part of this book has tried to sketch the pain of humanity, the death of hope and liberty in the lives of two-thirds of humanity. If the situation seems to echo a dying world, an unloved world, then the promise of the intimate and gentle Lord is that together we can love everything into life. We are great and beautiful, we are fire, we are his most precious gifts.

One of the most shining gifts to us was in the ragged person of Francis who loved everyone for no reason at all and whose prayer of action is perhaps the most simple.

All Shall Be Well

Make me your instrument of Peace,
where people are hating each other,
let me touch them with love,

Where people hurt, let me bring pardon,
where there is doubt in hearts, let my life
touch theirs with some faith.

Where people give up in despair, let my
humanness bring hope.

Where there is darkness, let me bring light.
Where people are sad let me bring joy.

God help me put others before me,
and open my eyes to the need all around me,
and see beyond myself into their hearts,
understand through me and console
them and take away stress and anxiety.

It is in giving that we receive,
It is in loving that we are given the richest
love, it is in forgiving that we truly
free ourselves from resentment and pettiness,

And when we die, we are released into the
fullest miracle of total loving, Amen.

To be a Christian, especially in today's world, is to be "giving" – giving of time, patience, humour, trust, listening. It is having time to talk to people, to share, to receive, to learn. To be a Christian is first to become a real human being, a real miracle, a uniquely alive, aware, opening being, taking pleasure in life, rejoicing in one's sexuality, not burying it, finding power in silence, not boredom, finding friends in strangers, not outsiders.

The Dynamic Response

Action does not necessarily mean all of us charging off to carry old ladies over roads or rushing off to Africa. It means doing your best with patience and self-understanding where you are. Sanctity is living the gift of God. It is dynamic in the fidelity of the little man saying his prayers in the back of the church, just as it speaks in a cry of "Help!" The key to life, the great secret, is realizing that we are not alone, we cannot be defeated.

The key is trusting him. In this lies the acid test of a living God in a living man, in washing the dishes, listening to music, dancing, and appreciating the countless gifts in others. Greatness lies not in the famous or important people, but in the simple and hidden love, quiet loyalty and fidelity, in the daily service of caring for each other.

Holiness lies in accepting the tenderness of God making divine the most mundane, making special the most ordinary. The sacred is when the smallest action done with care and compassion, no matter how unimportant it may seem, is done as a hymn, as a gift, as a promise of a new life in a new creation, and the dawn of that creation is us.

The "Yes" of life is translating the words of Scripture to my hands, to my body, to my touch, my caress, my work. Of course we still get hurt, we still know failure, we still get angry and have frustrated desires and needs, but everything will be seen in a different light from a new horizon, even though there are days when we get out of bed and don't really feel very much like a walking miracle, and there are times when it all just seems a bloody mess.

During the one and a half hours it takes to read this book, over 1,500 children under five will have died from malnutrition (UNICEF Annual Report 1984). Our humanity cries out for God to put an end to the torture and misery of millions in countries whose names fade quickly from the headlines.

All Shall Be Well

The dynamic response of life is essentially a silent and deeply intimate, personal familiarity with a forgiving and gentle God, but it is much more too.

> God has destined the world and everything in it for every-one. The goods of creation must flow into the hands of all men in just proportion, according to justice which is inseparable from charity ... All other rights of whatever kind ... must be subordinated to it. [They] must foster its achievement, and it is a grave and urgent social duty to restore them to their original aims.
> *(Populorum Progressio)*

Over the last twenty years, the Catholic Church has, especially in the Third and Fourth Worlds, identified itself with the poor and oppressed. It has been given extraordinary mandates by the documents of the Second Vatican Council who, in the original spirit of the carpenter's son, returned to the love of life, not the implementation of ritual and law. Encyclical letters such as *Evangelii Nuntiandi* spoke of all things being relative, the only absolute being the love of God.

The wealth of the Church, as St Lawrence put it, is the lost, the poor and the sick. It is our responsibility to serve them and restore justice by defending basic human rights. Silence becomes apathy; response means being prepared to stand up. "Shine before men, that they may see your good works and give glory to your Father who is in heaven" (Matthew 5:16).

The call to serve the poor and stand for their rights is not a call to armed rebellion to overthrow corruption. It is not violent or political. It is of God. Our actions, like our prayers, must be born from the matrix of human life. They must reflect the drama of life, but with a peace and trust that transfigures the most desperate, untenable situation into one of hope.

One of the most important things we can learn in this

The Dynamic Response

world is the philosophy of total and unconditional non-violence. With the tenderness of Christ and his call for love and sacrifice, we were challenged never to seek revenge, never hurt, never inflict pain, and when someone hurts us, to turn the other cheek.

It is so easy to rationalize violence, punishment and retribution. It is understandable to want to blow a man's brains out of his head if you know he wants to kill you. But we are clearly told: "Judge not, and you will not be judged" (Luke 6:37).

But Lord these men are murderers . . .

"But I say to you that hear, love your enemies, do good to those who hate you" (Luke 6:27).

These people abuse and persecute and hurt innocent people, should we just lie down and . . . ?

"Bless those who curse you, pray for those who abuse you" (Luke 6:28).

So you want me to just let him hit me. Some God you are. If he hits me I'll kick his face in . . .

"I know how you feel, I was there too. If someone hits you, let him hit you again. Love your enemies, and do good, and lend expecting nothing in return . . ." (Luke 6:35).

But Lord this doesn't make any real sense. Just look around you . . .

"Child, why do you call me 'Lord, Lord', and not do what I tell you?" (Luke 6:46).

It is easier not to do as he says. In anger we strike out. We beat up a wife, we hit our son over the head, we cane a frightened pupil. We shout, we bully, we vent our anger. Whether it be the emotional blackmail of moody silence, or banging around the house, or sarcasm and cynicism, it is all violence. A well-timed comment can be more damaging than a well-placed club. Violence is the tool of the defeated, the injured. There can never be any place for the love of God in a life that accepts or reasons on the use of violence. All violence is evil, all wars are unjust, all pain caused by man's inhumanity is the cause of global hatred and inequality.

To this day, in a supposedly stable society, corporal violence has not been stamped out of English schools. It has left its scars of distorted and unhealthy minds, a festering shadow of sadism, and an infringement of human dignity. We have a responsibility to respect each other, to protect and defend the weak, build a society that protects life and condemns all forms of violence.

"In the evening of our lives, we will be judged on love," said St John of the Cross. We will be judged not on our material success, not on pretences or role-plays, but on the quality and depths of our understanding and compassion.

But remember, Lord, I am not my brother's keeper. It's not my problem.

"True, my son. You are not your brother's keeper . . . But perhaps you are your brother's brother."

Of all the mystical and theological studies and tracts on love, none quite matches the clarity of Paul:

> Even if I am clever and brilliant and have a great way with words and have no love, something in me is cold and empty.
>
> And if I devote my life to the service of the poor and give all I have to feed the starving, and lay down my life, but have no love, then what's the point?
>
> Love endures all things, Love suffers long, it is always kind. Love is not jealous, Love is not out for display, it is not conceited or unmannerly, it is neither self-seeking or irritable.
>
> Love does not take account of any wrong that is suffered, it sees no joy in injustices, but comes from truth.

The Dynamic Response

Love bears everything in silence and has indomitable faith. Love hopes in every situation no matter how hopeless, and it endures without limit.

Love never fails, everything else in life will pass away . . .

Now we see unclearly, only in part. Then, we shall see him face to face . . . We will understand just as now we are understood.

Then after everything is gone and has passed away, there will only be three things left,

Faith, hope and love, and the greatest of these is love (1 Corinthians 13:1–13).

Only this love born of faith makes sense of the raging world around us. It draws its power from a living source and moves in us in concrete action, in subtle movements, in the most trivial of circumstances. This is the love of the almighty Father, who moved among us as man and rises in our lives as the boundless spirit of compassion and love.

When it came to discussing the love of God and trying to live it, I consulted a friend whose own personal life reflects much of what I am trying to say. He has spent a lifetime among the poor in Africa as a priest and teacher. Every day he encounters the most depressing human situations of squalor and poverty. He summarized what we have said with his characteristic style: "He came into the world, he loved us, promised us happiness and joy, he stretched out his arms, he was killed, he returned and is loving and calling us to love each other. The rest is mystery, that is all we know."

We live in hope of being loved, of being celebrated, of being helped. If we embrace the vision of Christ, he acts through us, healing, building, restoring, calling all his creation into a new and real life. We are Christ in the world, his children, his fire. The promise of the future lies in our faithfulness and in our determination to love the least of our brothers.

CHAPTER EIGHT

All Shall Be Well

There is much pain, many things that crush our dreams and hopes. We fail, we worry, we become afraid. The Promised Land seems very far away. Faith is hard because we are weak, we often lose hope and feel the love we give is inandequate, but **"All this is part of the mystery: All shall be well, all shall be well, Have no fear, for all manner of things shall be well"** (Mother Julian of Norwich, *Revelations of Divine Love*).

There is a story that tells of Julian of Norwich at the end of her life. A young soldier was telling her of the horrors of war and the cruelties he had seen. "How can you say everything will be well? Look how savage we can be, how the world hurts. Look at the blood on our swords, the stains in our hearts. You do not know how evil men can be . . ." Mother Julian replied: "Christ did not say you will not be tempted, you will not be hurt, you will not be afflicted, but he did say: 'You will not be overcome'."

I cannot stop wars, I cannot feed everybody, neither can I right the wrongs of the whole world. But perhaps I can change myself and bring joy into my little corner of the world. Mother Teresa was asked if her work in the slums of Calcutta was not a futile and hopeless waste of effort, just a drop in the ocean. "Perhaps," she replied, "but it is my drop, my humanity. Nothing is hopeless."

To let our humour, our kindness and patience shine out will make a better world. When we try to see what is good and beautiful in each other, what is wondrous, we are bringing hope and courage to those around us. I do not know why the poor are poor, I do not know why the world is so unequal, but I share the conviction that by loving and trying to serve, we can calm the troubled waters around us. When confronted with the cold realities of today's world, it is difficult to see even a glimmer of hope. Unless the rich countries stop exploiting the poor nations, the cycle of disease, famine, aid, and leaving the half-starved to subsist until the next famine, will spiral into renewed disasters. Unless we, as a whole, realize the enormous responsibilities we share, we will continue to give our brothers the crumbs off our table instead of sharing and redistributing what we have.

We are called upon to challenge what is wrong, to stand by what is true, to defend the voiceless. Whether it be the Church in Poland condemning oppression, or the English Bishops challenging Government policies in inner cities, or the unarticulated commitment in our hearts, we are called to challenge greed, hatred and apathy.

Ultimately there is no rationale or reasoning to explain the believer's standpoint. When the lights are switched off, the books are put away and I am alone, it must be me myself who says, "No matter what comes at me, no matter how bad things might appear, no matter what is said, I am with you, Lord. I trust in you, I want you, I love you. I know that at your side I am safe, nothing can overcome you. In you, all things will be well."

It was a time of plague and unrest. A delegation from the town was sent into the forest to consult the hermit who lived with God on the hill far away. At last they found him talking with the sparrows who were repairing the hermit's roof with straw. The deputation introduced itself and, sitting down, began to consult with the hermit.

"Do you know why God is sending this plague upon us?"
"No."
"Why is he not helping us to prosper? Why have we become so poor?"

"I don't know."

"Can you at least give us a sign, a proof, that God is there?"

"No."

"What *can* you give us?"

"Only what is already in your hearts – darkness; and in the darkness there will be light."

"We are sick."

"You will be healed."

"Our children have died!"

"They will rise again."

"But . . ."

"He will give you eyes to see, and hearts to love and trust him. Even if you cannot see the coming of the dawn, walk with him and have no fear."

While love may be a great ideal, we often fall far short of the goal. Most of us hustle and hassle, bark and tread on people's toes. Most people live sincerely trying to be better and nicer. We are committed to paying the bills, feeding the kids, pleasing the boss, calming family rows.

In many parts of the world the day to day bid for survival balances more on the edge of live or die, finding enough to feed the children, water to drink, something to keep away the cold at night, than on calming family rows. Whatever the situation, it is still hard ever to find enough time to listen to God, to see what is beautiful, to be still and let go. For some reason it seems an easier leap the poorer you are, and joy seems to dance more visibly among the poor than in the avenues of the rich.

We can do more than we are doing. We can care more, forgive more, trust more, we can find more giving in our hearts, more warmth. The more we begin to learn of the endless mystery of ourselves the more lovable and loved we become, and the more we realize how deeply God is alive in us and how beautiful life can become.

All Shall Be Well

I have seen a great deal of poverty, suffering and human pain. I have also seen most extraordinary deeds of sacrifice and selflessness. There is heroism and greatness all around us.

Initially I had contemplated a philosophical examination of the meaning of gentleness and kindness in a world of pain and need. The present text evolved into a simple act of hope. This book was written during the recent East African drought and therefore was interrupted many times by the reality around us.

If real life crashes through publishers' time schedules, so too does God. We have spoken of a loving Lord, but words so poorly reflect anything. There are many questions, many blank pages that are left unfilled.

In a divided world where none of us are immune to pain, it is hard to make sense of the chaos. We cannot pray over it, or duck under it, or bypass humanity in a shortcut to God and happiness. The only thing that matters, the only thing of absolute importance in our lives, is that we love each other, and when we fail, as we so often do, that we try to love again.

We would dry up and become empty very soon were it not for support and friendship. The well of love, the source of power, is, I believe, in the intimacy of a private and deeply personal nakedness to God. This God is already inside us breathing life into us, caressing and cherishing us.

A friend of mine once commented that if he were to die he would like to be remembered as a kind man, because kindness is what flows from love. In a rough world where the hurtful joke and unthinking word can hurt someone, where there's so much criticism and little charity, our gentleness is needed, our courage is wanted, above all, our human "yes" is needed. What counts is how we live, how we care, how hard we try. "Do you love me?" I will try, Lord. "Then feed my lambs."

And as we walk into the blaze of life, whatever may happen, His presence is there, His joy, and in our deepest selves, we know that, indeed, "All shall be well, all things shall be well, all manner of things shall be well."

Reflections and Prayers

Where does one begin in a world such as this?

We have closed the door on most of mankind, choosing not to look out at the seas of poor and outcast. There is simply no room for them in a world that wastes so much.

Where do we begin to lead human lives in a society so constrained? Where do we live honest lives?

We were meant to be gentle, born to be part of nature and to move slowly within a natural creative act of love. What has it become? An anxiety? A time of stress and depression? And humanity, mindless of its inwardness, has become buried in inanities, in platitudes, in hopeless illusions that occupy the emptiness.

Unless we see things as human beings part of the whole, we shall remain inept, dishonest and false. Life is about embracing the weak, the crushed and the broken. It is about us together as one family.

Instead, we have dog eating dog.

There, in the sum of life that she has been given,
The conditions in which she has struggled to find the Kingdom of God,
Rarely has she rested – or enjoyed comfort.
She has known hunger and deprivation, extreme poverty, dead children.
She thirsts, and in her rags is hungry.
She is quiet, but dignified.
She has nothing – only a smile.

All Shall Be Well

Let me serve you as Christ would,
Let me welcome you into my home always.
Let me be patient with you,
Let me clean your hands and wash your feet,
Let me dress your wounds and comfort your distress.
Let me wipe away your tears and rejoice with you in your happiness.
Let me hold you in my arms when there is nowhere else,
Let me free you to go where your heart calls.
Let me bring you joy. Let me serve you.

Service and compassion are the lifeblood of living trust and hope. Giving is the nature of love. Standing by the oppressed and defending justice is the basis of a true humanity. Helping each other without advertising what we are doing is real support. Just as God has given us everything for nothing, so too should we be prepared to work out of love and charity.

Nothing is stronger than love, nothing deeper, nor better in heaven or earth. Love is born of God and cannot rest anywhere but in God, beyond all created things. One who loves is borne on wings: he runs and is filled with joy, he is free and unrestricted. He gives all to receive all, and he has all in all; for beyond all things he rests in the highest thing, the source of love. Love has no measure, but burns white hot without measure. Love aspires to do more than its strength allows; it does not plead impossibility, but considers it can do all things. Love is wearied without exhaustion, wounded without being crushed, alarmed without being destroyed. Like a living flame or a burning torch, it leaps up and safely passes through all. When a man loves, he knows the meaning of that cry that sounds in the ears of God, "You are wholly mine, I am wholly yours."

Love is sincere and kind, wise and long-suffering, it

never seeks its own end, for where a man seeks his own end, he at once falls out of love. Anyone who is not prepared to endure everything and stand by the beloved is not worthy of the name "lover".

Thomas à Kempis, *The Imitation of Christ*
Book 3 chapter 5)

If we are not surrounded by people whose lives echo love and personal tenderness, if we are not in daily contact with sensitivity and warmth, parts of our personhood become arid and crippled.

Without affection, we become emotionally and personally stunted because it is the nature of human beings to desire and long for a consistent bond of love. The bounds of our society prevent us from being the complete and whole people we desire to be.

Just as a plant withers and dies in dry ground, so too we slowly wither and die if our roots do not reach deep enough through the darkness and into the light of a hidden source.

We are fragile, each of us, insecure, and restored only by the origin of our lives – made whole again only by the very reason for our life which is a love that reaches into the hearts of the most adandoned and forgotten.

Is it true that love takes away our fears, but so too can fear bury love. Only love that flows from the source overcomes fear, only love given from God survives the ravages of life. The only everlasting love is born in the dark night, when the soul feels the heaving and the brooding of a deeper life within. Only God is love, and when we love, he is in us.

Holiness is simply how we live with each other, it is the

kindness and mercy we give. It is the happiness and joy we generate, it is the patience and humour we have. Holiness is hands outstretched in welcome and enfolded in love. It is the awakening of Christ into all we do, and even in weakness and failure it is our fidelity to his hidden will.

Joy isn't seeing the happy things in life, but seeing the presence of God in all the things around us.
Each act becomes important,
Each day a new miracle,
Each person, a gift from God to love.
Joy is measuring your days by the fire of his touch, not by success and failure.
Joy is coming alive to what is within and beginning to see the Promised Land. It is the dream becoming true in you.
Joy is the presence of a loving God.

Lovers or friends desire two things. The one is to love each other so much that they enter into each other and only make one being. The other is to love each other so much that having half the globe between them their union will not be diminished in the slightest degree.

Simone Weil

Failure is impossible to those who love.
  Everything ceases to be measured in human terms, and we see ourselves in the light of one truth.
  That gentleness, compassion and love shall overcome all else.

It does not matter when we die, only that before we pass into the hands of God, we have lived the fullness of life.

Reflections and Prayers

How many years we live is significant, only that in the time given we have tried with all our hearts to love.

Very slowly, in the ruins of the human soul, do we begin to see a great light. From the ashes of failure and broken dreams, within our greatest defeats, is born amid the trembling, a hope, and in the deep dark there comes from out of the rubble, new love, new joy, an inexplicable presence from nowhere. This is the spirit of a living God healing, making whole the fragile child created by his hand. As surely as we breathe, so too does he enfold every precious moment of our lives.

> Let nothing disturb thee,
> Let nothing afright thee.
> All things are passing,
> God alone is changeless.
> Patience gains all things.
> Who hath God wanteth nothing.
> For alone God sufficeth.
> *St Teresa of Avila*

Lord, Here I am, head bowed, a little anxious and uneasy and, once again, a little lonely.

I feel very depressed amid all the chaos and busyness I see around me. Somehow I even feel drawn by it all, the comfort, security and prestige. I know you want so much more, but what you ask is unfair. It is easy to fail, and so they have rewritten what you have said. It's easier that way. It's more comfortable.

I don't want to see any lonely, depressed people or poor, desperate neurotics. I want good-looking friends who laugh and enjoy each other. I like the excitement and warmth of good company and really you aren't much fun to be with. With you, I seem to meet man at his weakest and most crushed. You are not really very helpful when I'm

All Shall Be Well

down and when I'm sad. You never talk to me or touch me. I need you to speak to me through those around me. I need some gentleness too, a smile, a glance, a presence, an embrace. You have called me to love, but I am human and need human love as well. Out there, what you have created does not want to know you or hear about you. They have distorted what you said. Where are we to begin? Should we even bother?

You give us something they can do well without, so why don't you leave us alone and admit that it was a terrible mistake. Why don't you open your eyes to all this pain, this loneliness? They want to love and yet they can't. Where are we going? What have we become? Where are you?

It seems so dark and all around me, amid the giggles and grins, I see your children crying out but you aren't there.

When grace is lost from life and all is tired and empty in my soul; when I am wasted and defeated – come whisper to me.

When angered and enraged and left alone, and this your son is sad and hurt; when I have failed you and lie buried in the din – enfold my weeping soul.

When I am crushed in shame, trembling in my pain, bereft of hope, in dark despair, alone – then, gentle Lord, come then and move within. Move me, enfold me in eternity and with your light and thunder, cast from me my fears. Kiss and make me new.

Out of the depths I cry to you, O Lord, and you never answer me.

I try so often to reach you and hear only my own imaginings. Why are you so difficult to touch?

Reflections and Prayers

I can't reach you, so please touch me, find me, come to me. Teach me how to open to you because I can't do this by myself.

In my prayer,
I am frustrated.

In my silence,
I am bored.

In my thoughts,
I am drowned.

In my turmoil,
I am hurt.

In my loving,
I find little in me to give.

What am I doing wrong, Lord?

Little one,
Let me pray in you, let me be your silence.
Let me lift up your thoughts.
I will still the storm, and in your hands I will place my children to be loved. In your eyes I will speak, and my words shall be in your mouth. You shall be my dwelling place and through you I shall cast joy upon the earth.

But, God, I feel so bad, so...

Nothing I have made is bad, you are everlasting.
You are mine.

What a bloody world we have, Lord, so full of increasing

violence and pain. Men are capable of such terrible cruelties and you stand by as the old are beaten and the innocent murdered.

Have you deserted us and left us? We are weak and frightened of being left alone. It all seems so useless, Lord, and I feel helpless to heal anything.

I do not know how to pray, I peer into a foreign realm, tired by the needs of this world.

In my weakness and troubled search, find me; in my uselessness, use me; in the darkness reach out and take my trembling hand.

I cannot see you,
I cannot hear you,
I cannot find you.
Words do not comfort me, only your touch can heal me. When I am anxious and worried, please be here. When my stomach turns and I panic, hold me. When I deny you and desert you, whatever I do, be with me and remember I am only as strong as you make me. Do what I cannot do, heal what I cannot heal, bring hope where I cannot and love when my heart is empty.

Lord, Fill me with sincerity and nakedness. Open my eyes to the suffering around me. Let your love flow inside me into the lives of all I meet.

I feel your breath, you, pure and hidden, apart yet forever within.

Dwell inside me. Darkness is shattered by your touch and in the ocean of solitude I have found you moving in the depths. I am empty, fill me. When I abandon you, forgive me. I will fail you, I will hurt you, I will desert you. My very actions will betray and I will wander far from you. Yet in my weakness come to me and lift me when I fall, because the world is very frightening and lonely without you.

Open inner eyes to inner stillness, that I can see the

Reflections and Prayers

beauty of your ways, in sight beyond seeing and knowing beyond what is. O Lord, may I may live your dream into reality.

How often I think I understand you, then my images are shattered. I want to love you, I want to be worthy of my God, but it's so hard to love someone you cannot even see. Gentle one, only you know what is inside my heart. You know my moods and sins, my secrets and fears. Only you know the whole me, and yet you still love me.

I stand before you now, your child. Lift me in your arms and burn bright within me for ever, through your beautiful and tender Son and his spirit of gentleness and love.

Lord, we thank you for the honour of serving you in your distressing disguise and for the privilege of being with you. Teach us to give more and more again, and when we have nothing to give, pour your love inside us, and open our hearts.

Teach us to serve you as you deserve. To give and not to count the cost, to fight and not to heed the wounds, to toil and not to seek for rest, to labour and not to seek for any reward save knowing that we do your will.

St Ignatius Loyola

Bibliography

Very few people read through a rigid list of books. But here are a few suggestions that have helped many people to think more deeply and love more fully.

Human living

For insight into human pain and the human search, and for common sense and honesty, try reading the books of Father John Powell, S.J.: *Why Am I Afraid to Love?*, *Why Am I Afraid to Tell You Who I Am?*, and *The Secret of Staying in Love*. His study of faith is important in *A Reason to Live, A Reason to Die*. Perhaps his most beautiful book is *He Touched Me*, on his own very human search for a God of love.

The Art of Loving by Erich Fromm is a masterpiece, simply written.

Inspiration

There are many great works that reveal new things. The work of Mother Teresa of Calcutta in *Something Beautiful for God* is one such book. Another, that only seems to touch willing hearts, is *Mr God, This is Anna* by Fynn. The Short Stories of Oscar Wilde will amaze you.

Christ

I can think of no better writing on Christ than the Gospels. On his intimacy and gentleness, *The Last Temptation* by Nikos Kazantzakas is one of the finest books ever written. Many of Michael Quoist's writings are also on the subject of Christ.

All Shall Be Well

The Inner Life

The Practice of the Presence of God by Brother Lawrence and *The Little Way* of St Thérèse of Lisieux are written by simple people from their direct experience, in a style free from specialist terms or concepts.

Inward Stillness by George Maloney, together with his book *Bright Darkness*, are very helpful, as is van Breeman's book, *As Bread That is Broken*.

Poustinia by Catherine de Hueck Doherty has been used and adapted by thousands in their daily prayer life, and Thomas Merton's *Seeds of Contemplation* casts light on the nature of contemplation. For those interested in understanding more about Eastern Methods, Dechanet's books on the spiritual aspects of yoga are invaluable, and *Silent Music* by William Johnston is both personally enriching and informative on Zen.

For ideas on what to meditate about, *The Song of the Bird* by Anthony de Mello, S.J. has many beautiful stories carefully collected and presented for that purpose.

Love is All by J. L. Bird, and *The Pain of Being Human* by Eugene Kennedy, are downtoearth and helpful. The application of the Christian ideal comes out in *Religion and Personality* by Adrian van Kaam.

The Dark Night of the Soul by St John of the Cross discusses some of the deeper aspects of the inner spiritual life. *The Fire of Love* by Richard Rolle is also readable.

The most readable and often most moving of Teilhard de Chardin's books is *Prayer of the Universe* which opens the door of prayer into a cosmic reality in Teilhard's overall vision of the universe. Also suggested is *Markings* by Dag Hammarskjöld.

For prayerful reading, *Instrument of Thy Peace* by Alan Paton is excellent. *Thoughts of Solitude* by Thomas Merton is full of encouragement and ideas. This is also true of *The Cloud of Unknowing* (Anon).

Even for the atheist, a must is Andrew Greeley's disturbing and challenging *The Great Mysteries*, in which he deals with the dilemma of human pain and the growth of inner life.

Everything can feed instead of distract the inner life of man, all we need is the will. Books such as *Auschwitz* by Dr Miklos Nyisli and *Famine: A Man-Made Disaster* by the Independent Commission on Human Issues only serve to encourage us to pray and to serve. *The Reflections of St Bernard* and *The Flowers of St Francis* make perfect sense of it all.

The list is rich and these are but a few of a great wealth of writings that speak of a better, happier world of light and love and compassion. One book that must not be overlooked is pure magic: *The Prophet* by Kahlil Gibran.

The mystical traditions of both the early Christian Church and Vedic schools contain many rich sources – and many words of wisdom, among them one other reference, "To find the secret of love, read in the book of your heart, upon the pages of your soul, in the words of His hand."